*Raimondo an
I thong
a copy - Sorry you waited. I hope
you're not disappointed...
Vin D'Aleo*

Fifty Steps

Vincent L D'Aleo

Copyright © 2012 Vincent L D'Aleo
All rights reserved.
ISBN: 1467903574
ISBN 13: 9781467903578

Table of Contents

Stories	Page Number
CHILDHOOD	
Dawn	3
007	9
Old Testament	15
Chutes and Ladders	21
Breakfast	25
An Optimal Learning Environment	33
Sixty-One	39
Community Standards	43
Currier and Ives	47
In the Good Ole Summertime	53
Scratch and Sniff	57
Young Sinatra	61
Spurs and Sixguns	69
Where Have You Gone, Chuck Taylor?	73
Diners Club	77
Yin and Yikes	81
GPS	87
For the Want of a Nail	93
FRIENDSHIP, MARRIAGE, and CHILD-REARING	
Baby Steps	99
Mr. Lucky	103

Island Hopping 109
Sharing the Sandbox 113
Justifiable Homicide. 117
Measuring Up. 121
Dolce Fa Niente. 125
Wallpaper 129
Yalta 133
Detailed Instructions Not Enclosed. 139
Revelations 143
Kodak Moment 147
Parents' Weekend 151
The ABCs. 157
Paternity 161
BFF 165

TRAVEL and OTHER THINGS
Monkey Shovels 171
Baggage Claim 175
The OK Corral 179
Shameless Exhibitionism 183
Nine-Tenths of the Law 187
Snow Days. 191
Indian Head Pennies. 195
Stacking Toast 199
The Louisiana Purchase 205
Tofu 209
Steal a Cadillac 211
Lost and Found. 215
Unholy Wedlock 221
Driving at Night 225
Character Flaws. 229
The Best and the Brightest 233
Capital Punishment 237
Fifty Steps 241

CHILDHOOD

Dawn

I think it's fair to say that I was an agreeable fetus and embryo. There's no reason to think otherwise. The child is father to the man, and I believe I'm an agreeable man too. At my birth, I wasn't awkwardly large, not wanting to inconvenience my mother. She had graciously hosted me for nine months, and in all good taste, I wouldn't have betrayed that generosity. As a matter of fact, I was just under seven pounds, the ideal size for a baby. In keeping with the times, my mother gained just over seven pounds during her pregnancy, a kind of save-the-planet thinking that was clearly ahead of the times.

Not only did I keep my weight in check, but I chose to be born at a time when women giving birth entered the hospital, were thrown into unconsciousness and presented with their bundle of joy some hours after the anesthesia wore off. I know that today's soccer-driving, treadmill-running moms have a different idea of how to give birth, but my way was far more civilized.

Don't ask me how I know all this. It's more like putting together pieces of memories—hearing stories, looking at the parts of me now that I can't explain, and filling in those blanks. Anyway, it works best if I call these memories and leave it at that.

I was a precocious child. I walked very early, at eight months, and was talking before that. Not just talking, but singing. My favorite was "Goodnight Irene." I won't go so far as to say that I knew every verse, just the first stanza and the chorus. I liked other songs, too, but this was my number one by a mile..

My mother didn't find my singing unusual. She was very quiet herself, but there was no doubt that she was proud of me. One of her sisters was bragging that her year-old son knew a dozen words. I knew a dozen adjectives to describe the family dog (and, to be honest, the dog was pretty boring). I realize now that being blessed with a child like me could have resulted in complications. What could she say that wouldn't hurt feelings? As it turned out, that cousin had a solid career running a waste dump in Wyoming. All's well that ends well.

Until I was just under two, we lived in a one-room cold-water flat. These days we'd call it a studio. You can charge more that way, but this place was not romantic enough to carry that off. It was over a bar, a respectable one, with a ladies' entrance. After all, we had an image to uphold.

Our lodging was only temporary, of course. My father was building our house during the day, and that took time. It might have gone more quickly if anyone could stand to work with him, but that would have meant that he would have had to share his plans with someone else. They weren't secret, you understand. He just didn't like to take the time to explain what he was doing. No matter that this resulted in his building an entire house virtually alone. I think he liked it that way.

To be perfectly honest, there was one man who helped him once in a while. Although I was under two, I remember him vaguely. His name was Red something or other. He must have been forty, but he might have been sixty, I couldn't tell. He liked to smoke cigarettes on newly shingled roofs, an odd characteristic that still plays largely in my mind..

When I was two, we moved from the room into our house. It wasn't completely ready, but our room had developed a rodent problem that my mother couldn't tolerate; so into our new almost-house we went. The house smelled of wood and freshly plastered walls. In the soon-to-be living room, my father projected my shadow on a bare wall with a droplight and traced my silhouette. Because of that silhouette, I can say with certainty that I was singularly handsome. It stayed on that wall in place of wallpaper for years. It was a sad day for me when we could finally afford to cover it over.

Eventually, the house was finished. Well, perhaps that's not quite accurate. It was never really finished while my father was alive. He had too many ideas and too much energy to leave well enough alone. Our weekends were an unending series of improvements and additions, none of which seemed necessary to anyone but him.

I'm getting ahead of myself. That particular set of miseries is for another time. We had an old Chevy, a '36, I think. It had running boards that were excellent to play on, and it had the first set of license plates I ever memorized. I was about three, and my parents felt that this was more evidence of the exceptional intelligence I possessed. I never told them that it was a trick. I hadn't memorized it at all. The plate number was VT495, and the first and last letters of my name were V and T. I was born in 1949, and 4 and 9 were the first two digits in the plate. I really only had to remember the final five. It was easy.

I hadn't yet told them that I could read. I didn't want to upset them.

In the hallway outside of my parents' room, there hangs a photo of me at that age. It was one of those posed pictures, taken by Olin Mills or some other studio. It was black and white, but "colorized," as was the way in those days. In it, I'm sitting on the floor, wearing dress pants, a white shirt, and a bow tie. I don't suppose it's necessary to say that I was cuter than cute.

They posed me with an open book in my hands, although I was looking at the camera. I really didn't have to focus on the book, a barnyard favorite titled *Why Roostie Crowed*, because I had read it enough to commit it to memory. It was a genre I favored very much in those days: animals with peculiarities that needed explaining. I had solved the mystery of why the nuts disappeared from the back steps (squirrels), ideal construction techniques for porcine residences (brick), how to get supper if you're a kitten (don't lose your mittens), and who would help to plant the wheat (no one). Reading was for me.

The Felician sisters finally noticed this when I was three and a half and had already progressed to the classics. *On Beyond Zebra* was a mindblower, opening up possibilities of worlds beyond my perception, a revelation that might have stood me in good stead later on with the Jesuits at Boston College, if ennui and alcohol hadn't intervened. Once again, a story for later.

Anyway, I went to nursery school right about at that time. The sisters were a mixed lot, and I quickly sized them up. Sister Mary Michael was one of those young ones who still thought children had a chance at heaven. I tried to stick close to her. Sister Angelina was at least a thousand years old and was convinced that her job was to keep the hounds of hell busy for four hours a day, until their incompetent parents could come and pick them up and spoil them some more.

My earliest memory of the treachery of adults was of Sister Angelina putting some poor kid behind the door as we trouped outside for our time in the sun. Whatever capital felony this boy had committed must have been horrendous. His eyes met mine as I peeked out from behind Sister Mary Michael. No words were exchanged, but in that instant I knew that innocence was no protection from the wrath of frustrated adults, a lesson that has remained true without exception for the last fifty-seven years. I was also introduced to the curious qualities of moral ambivalence. I felt terrible for my brother behind the door, yet wildly grateful that it wasn't me. While it did little to make me a better grown-up, all in all, nursery school was full of important developmental learning.

Things at home were getting more complicated right about then too. The way I see it, my obvious talents were becoming a threat to my father, who began to feel the need to establish his dominance in the household. I had developed a love of Robin Hood, indirectly stemming from dad's quest for the most advanced technology available. We had a television when it was still exotic. In those days, you could invite people over to watch TV and they would be flattered and excited. Your mother would put out the best ashtrays. Your guests would put on their best clothes and bring a tuna noodle casserole. The television was a piece of furniture, not some unobtrusive flat screen, but a Buick-sized box with a slightly oval-shaped window where the magic happened.

At four I still was allowed some time to sit by myself while Dad banged away in the basement. No parent in their right mind thought that watching television was a bad idea. Anything that kept the kid out of your hair was sensibly considered a valuable asset. One day, the Million Dollar Movie was *The Adventures of Robin Hood*, with Errol Flynn.

My life was changed. Never before or since did I have a more clear idea of who I was meant to be. Heroic and handsome, kind but capable of great violence, Hood/Flynn was the "me" I was destined to become. Somehow, my father recognized the rapture and made me a sword. It was a wooden beauty, with a whittled pommel, a strong but graceful hilt, and a straight, symmetrical blade. I'm virtually positive that it was the sword after which Excalibur was modeled.

All was well in my world. I had negotiated the razor reefs of nursery school, Mom loved me, books were my window into worlds unexplored, and now I was armed. Whenever things seem this perfect, watch out. My downfall came in the late afternoon. We had gone out in the Chevy; where, I don't know. We were on our way back into the house and as we crossed the front yard toward the door, I swung my mighty blade and decapitated the new blue spruce my father had just planted. To my dad, the six inches I removed were the most important six inches in the world. Catastrophe. Confrontation. Defeat.

The offshoot was being grounded for two weeks. In fact, no one talked about being grounded in those days, but that's what it amounted to: no television, in bed right after dinner. I was a four-year-old in solitary. It should be noted that even when I wasn't grounded, I went to bed right after dinner, and except for Saturdays and *Rootie Kazootie*, television was pretty bleak, but the idea that I was coming in second in a battle of wills was shocking. It was my introduction to the Sacre du Printemps, and I was the losing ram. Two weeks at four was like twenty years at forty, but even that time passed.

Kindergarten was less than a blur. I started at four, was given some sort of test, and next thing I knew I was a first-grader. I learned later that with the evil Soviets breathing down our necks, people with brains like mine were needed. They took six of us, declared us advanced, and planted us in groups with twenty-nine other drooling young minds eager for learning.

I myself excelled in a lot of things, but blocks were far and away my favorite. They had a huge box of them—wooden blocks of five or six different shapes. They were kept in a nook with a perfect open space in front and a flat rug that was just big enough for me and my friend Herbert. We would sit in silence, placing an arch atop two cubes, building walls and turrets that mimicked the castle from Disneyland. Sadly, there was never enough time to build everything I wanted, and here I learned another of life's great lessons: the more you like something, the less of it you get. Miss Rossini, our teacher (who had also taught my father; not a good sign!) had an almost supernatural talent for stopping playtime just as things began to take shape.

I got desperate enough to apply myself to the other things she wanted us to do, in the hope that I could satisfy her and go back to my construction. The ideas of reason and justice die hard, but Miss Rossini was a hard woman. No matter how quickly I finished (with little error, I might add), the blocks were often put away, and worse than that, she let other kids play with them.

There I tasted the humiliation of self-betrayal in the interest of pursuing my dream. I revealed my soul in the hope that the world would treat me fairly—and had that hope dashed. It was the beginning of the world weariness that was grammar school. There was the tragic affair that never was with Miss Schultz in third grade. (She betrayed me for Mr. Colarusso, the bald music teacher) and the torrid walk home with Linda Morris, complete with cupcakes made by her mother. No moment, though, stayed as true as the knowledge that the world resents the gifted and does its best to bring them down.

Thank goodness for the seventies, when the concept of "sticking it to the man" emerged to help me recover my self-esteem and gain a modicum of revenge. That again is another story for another time.

007

From my mother I learned stealth. I learned to be silent, and to endure. She learned these things early on in her life. Born on a farm in rural Pennsylvania, she was the eighth of ten surviving children born to her mother, Hattie Corson, and her father, John Harbst. My grandmother had married my thirty-two-year-old grandfather when she was sixteen. Her sister married his brother. She died on Christmas Eve of kidney failure after her last baby was born. She was thirty-six and my mother was six.

I've heard little about my grandmother's life. I have a photograph of her, standing in front of the farmhouse, neither smile nor scowl on her face, just the face of a woman used to hard work and the outdoors. They had no electricity or running water, and if the boys forgot to carry any from the spring, she had to get it herself. The story goes that she carried a .22 rifle as she went, and shot rattlesnakes that lived in the old stone walls along the path. A shoebox filled with those rattles was found beneath her bed after she died.

Life on the farm must have been interesting. My grandfather worked in a steel mill in the town and came home on weekends. My grandmother ran the farm and raised the kids while he was away. My uncles were a rough-and-tumble lot, and my grandfather was a practical man. If the boys' chores weren't done when he got home, they got a whipping. He didn't bother to sort out whether or not any one boy shirked their duties more than the others; he left that up to them. Boys' chores done, no problem—not done, a whipping.

It happened that my Uncle Frank was a lazy one. He knew the other boys would have to pick up his slack. They fought over it, I'm sure, but there was no budging Frank. His brothers, Earl and Jess, found a way to get satisfaction. They took my grandmother's precious cooking chocolate and melted it around neat balls of horse manure. Then they wrapped them up in fancy doilies and put them in a package. They addressed it to Frank from his latest girlfriend.

Frank wasn't just lazy, he was selfish. He took his box and went up the hill where he could eat in peace. The results are a family legend. For the rest of the week, the three brothers spent so much time fighting that none of the boys' chores got done. No chores and a whipping—but Earl and Jess thought it was worth it.

I'm sure my aunts weren't exactly delicate flowers. Susie, in particular, was given to drama. She was so small that even after she was married with two children, she could get into the movies as under the age of twelve. She claimed to be my grandfather's favorite, although that was never proven. She maintained that when the schoolteacher slapped her hand (a pretty mild punishment by most standards of the day), my grandfather went to the school with a buggy whip and beat the teacher. As I said, she was prone to drama, but the flavor of the story remains. They were a rough lot.

When my grandmother died, her family kind of collapsed. My uncles Earl and Frank had left the farm and joined the Army. For them, Army life was a vacation. My aunts Susie and Beulah had married and were on their own. The six little ones needed homes. The baby, Richard, was put up for adoption. I didn't even know he existed until my mother heard that he was killed in a car crash in the early 1960s. The five others were sent to live with various friends and family members while my grandfather continued to work and send money for their upkeep.

My mother and her brother Phillip stayed together. She was six and he was a year or so younger. From that time until she was a teenager, she didn't stay for a whole year in one home. They were shuttled from place to place, with some bearable and others hellish. I only know about any of this because in my fifty nine years I've listened closely and pieced it together bit by bit. But there are many gaps.

Sometime around age thirteen, my mother became Catholic. In that part of Pennsylvania during those times, that was like becoming Martian. I don't know for sure what brought about this conversion, but I have a story that I think I heard and that makes sense in light of my mom's secret ways. The story is that she was living with her oldest sister, Beulah, who had four children and was on a farm of her own. Her kids were getting old enough to be thinking of leaving the farm, and she needed help. She had four more babies, and she wanted my then thirteen-year-old mother to stop going to school to help with them.

My mother ran away and was caught. As punishment, they placed her in a "Nun School," where she prayed a prayer for some undetermined wish, and it was granted. Thus her faith was born. I don't know if this story is true. I don't even know if I heard it or if I made it up so long ago that it now seems sort of true. With my mother, you just don't know.

She ended up in Connecticut when she was eighteen, living with my aunt Lena, who was just a little older than she was, and married. By this time, my mother was pathologically shy and close to gorgeous. She looks most like the old actress Barbara Stanwyck, classy and aloof.

In a small town, there are usually places where people go to hang out. In Thompsonville right after World War II, that place was the Sugar Bowl. It was owned by a slick local guy named Joe Pork Chops, and everyone who was anyone filtered through every day. My mother got a job there as a waitress. Hard work was something she understood, but she wasn't so keen on the loose banter that circulated the place. She developed a reputation for being "stuck up," and given that it allowed her to go about her business without too much tension, she lived with it.

My father was her polar opposite in many ways. His lack of shyness eventually got through, and that's all she wrote. They were married for about thirty-five years when he died in 1984.

For all the years of their marriage, I never heard them argue. That might sound like a testament to a good marriage, but I'm not so sure. I think it might more accurately point to Mom's overwhelming aversion to conflict. My father wasn't an easy man to get along with. It took some doing to agree with him for thirty-five minutes, let alone years, but I can't remember ever hearing them argue.

I've begun to understand this gradually in the years since he died. The first clue was in the weeks after his funeral. My parents' house was filled with antiques. Glassware and clocks, Victorian furniture and musical instruments—you name it, it was there. My mother called my sister and me and said to come home. When we arrived, she swept her arm around and said, "If there's anything here you want, take it. Your father worked hard, he didn't drink, beat me, or cheat, but he loved junk. I've lived with this stuff for as long as he was alive. Now it's going. Take what you want." I never had an inkling that she didn't love antiques as much as he did. I'm sure my father didn't either.

Many people around my age would say that was the way of it for many wives in those days, and they would be right, but never to the degree that it existed for my mother. She could be on fire, and if she didn't want you to know about it, she'd cook you dinner, make you coffee, and you'd never know. Don't get the impression that she's a suffering saint, either. She takes no pleasure in recounting her aches and pains. She's no queen of guilt. My mother is just a woman who has lived her life with her mouth shut.

My sister and I were always told that "if you can't say something nice, don't say anything," but Mom could take this to the extreme. About twenty years ago, she had surgery to clean out her carotid artery. It's a delicate but common operation that involves opening up the artery, scraping it clear of buildup, and patching it up with a piece of vein from a leg.

After she returned home, that patch on her artery burst. It was four in the morning, and Mom noticed a lump building under her stitches. She got up and got dressed. She put on a Hermes scarf, and waited. My Aunt Lena lived next door to her, and went over at eight to see how she was doing. Over coffee, she noticed the scarf and then the lump, which was by then the size of a tennis ball. Horrified, she asked why Mom hadn't said anything. "The doctor's office isn't open until ten" was her reply. My aunt rode with her in the ambulance, and I'm sure saved her life.

Where did her example take me? I'm considered by most to resemble my father. I can be outgoing, and I like attention. I look more like him than I do her, so the assumption is easy to understand. What people don't know is that I have secrets. Just like her, I have the irrational feeling that if someone were to really know everything about me, they'd be shocked. Now, in my head I know that I'm about as exotic as peanut butter. I also know that you can't be married for thirty years and have real secrets. (Unless, of course, you're a serial killer leaving bodies buried in your neighbor's backyard.)

I also hate conflict and have had to work hard to overcome the belief that you have to make everything feel okay, even if it absolutely doesn't. I joke with my wife, Marcie, that, because of her, we never sit at the first table we're given in a restaurant. But they could sit me in a pool of sharks and I'd thank them for the opportunity to get a sharkskin suit.

Somewhere in the middle, there's peace.

My mother has shown extraordinary strength to live the life she was given and to make of it what she has. She's loved by more people than I can count, who go to her for help, company, and good humor. She's an old lady now, but I know some of the roads she's traveled, and though she made mistakes like the rest of us, god knows where most people would be in her shoes.

Old Testament

I talk a lot about my father. I don't suppose that's unusual. A man's father is the model he carries within him for a lifetime. The way that I tend to picture mine is similar to the picture of Moses in the Bible as he comes down from the mountain, carrying the Ten Commandments. The stone tablets seem weightless in his arms. His beard is flowing, and his face is set with righteousness. He is a man completely sure of himself. There is no doubt in him as to what is right and what is wrong. My father was that way too. I never saw shades of gray in him. He spoke in absolutes, and I listened as if his words were carved in stone.

Actually, my father loved to build with stone. In the late 1940s, he owned a bowling alley. There was no air-conditioning in those days, so it was closed during the heat of summer. He used the days as he wished and opened the alleys at night. He was young and strong, full of energy and independence. He'd really been on his own in his father's house since he was fifteen, and his mother took most of his eight brothers and sisters to New York City to get medical treatment for his youngest sister.

My dad loved to build things and was good at it. On his own, he built the house I grew up in and in which my mother still lives. It took him two years of summer days, working alone, but he did it. I think he liked the feeling of self-sufficiency he got from doing it himself.

He learned stone work from an old Italian man he met on one of his summer days. There had been a fire that burned St. Patrick's Church in the center of old Thompsonville, the section of Enfield, Connecticut, in which we both grew up. For days he'd stopped to watch the workers as they rebuilt the stone building. There were usually gawkers at the site, and he noticed one man there day after day. In the course of watching, Dad struck up a conversation with him and immediately discovered that he spoke no English. He was an Italian immigrant, a marble cutter, son of a marble cutter, grandson of marble cutters, and so on through more generations than he could count.

He stared as the workers placed stone on stone, unable to get work because he had no way to communicate with the foremen on-site. My father spoke Italian in his home and quickly made the connections the man needed. He was responsible for the marble altar and columns in the church that stands today. I'm sure no one remembers his name or his story, but I do. I remember because he repaid my father by teaching him how to set stones for walls and fireplaces, foundations and chimneys. Our home had four fireplaces. The room in which I slept for the years my grandfather stayed with us has a fireplace in it, a legacy of my father's love.

Stone is an unforgiving medium. It stays rigid and allows little alteration in its shape or nature. A man can chip away at a corner or shatter a slab, but it's usually better to find ones that fit each other as nature formed them. When we try to bend it to our purposes, it can crumble into uselessness or remain adamant, wearing out our intentions.

My father was both stone and shaper of stone. Having been formed by the forces of the world in which he lived, he found his niche and stayed there. He was the one to whom people went with questions, the arbiter of struggles, the solver of problems. God help the person who went to him hoping for less than the harsh truth. His words weren't often meant to appease.

He quit school in the eighth grade, which wasn't rare in the early 1930s. What was unusual was the manner in which he left. One afternoon, his teacher left the room. Before she did so, she warned the class to behave in her absence. Naturally, as soon as she left, the class began to do all the silly things eighth-graders do when the teacher is away. The problem was that the teacher wasn't away for nearly enough time. She reentered the room right in the middle of the tumult.

Sternly she demanded, "Is this the way you act when my back is turned?"

"Yes," my father answered.

"I didn't need you to tell me that," she said.

"Then why did you ask?" he replied.

That was the last day he attended school. It made no sense to him to spend time on this sort of thing. He went to work in his family's store, cared for two of his younger brothers, and was on his own.

My parents married in 1947. My father was thirty-two and my mother ten years younger. He had lived as he wished, for the most part, working many jobs, cultivating all kinds of relationships, and generally raising hell. He went to the race track and to the fights. He played pool and wore hats with the brim bent over one eye. He ran with fast crowds and kept up with all of them.

Marriage didn't change him, but it did change the way that he expressed his inner nature. There was no thought to his being a partner in marriage. His was the old Italian model of family, led by the patriarch. My mother was an extremely shy beauty, with no capacity for challenging authority. Their relationship suited him perfectly.

My father approached fatherhood in the same way that he approached anything else. He was the shaper, and I was the stone. It was his responsibility to form me as he saw fit, and here is where problems began. Not all stone is the same. Some cleaves cleanly when struck; some shatters like glass. A master mason knows that each piece has its own character and is best handled as it would want to be handled. My father was not a master mason. He was a gifted man, spectacularly talented in many ways. If he'd had the benefit of education, if he hadn't been raised Italian during the Great Depression, who knows what he could have become. As it was, he was a successful business man, a skilled builder, a watchmaker in his spare time, a politician, confessor to many, and a father.

Today I can look back on our relationship with perspective. He's been dead for more than twenty-five years. I'm a father myself. I think I can see past the Old Testament robes, into my father's heart.

When he was happy, my dad would rub his huge hands together and clap them. He'd take my mother, sister, and me out for a ride to Holyoke and get hot dogs at a place he'd gone to for decades. He told us the same stories every time, about how the owner started selling these hot dogs from a cart and about how they were made from a special recipe.

There was a jukebox in the restaurant, and if you put a nickel in, a small mechanical band played instruments as your song was sung. My sister and I would always play "Tom Dooley" and watch as they prepared our food.

In typical fashion, we weren't allowed to get chocolate milk. Dad knew it was a scam, because they used non-fat milk to make it. During the Depression, fat was a luxury, and stone once shaped doesn't easily allow change.

When he was happy, he'd tell stories. I loved those times when he was talking to one of his old friends, relaxed and happy in his own home, gracious and smooth. He was a master storyteller with a lifetime of memories. I seldom was at ease with him, but at those moments, I was in heaven. Always proud to be his son, at those moments, I could imagine that he might be a little proud of me.

I was not the same stone as he. I wasn't sure of myself, and I thought that was my nature. I wasn't an anvil stone on which other stones conformed or broke. I tried all too hard to fit the niches he left in his wake, and that stymied him. He wanted to force me into the form he thought best to cope with the world into which he was born. His goal was to foster confidence and strength, but his way was to demand it. I know better, but perhaps can't do better. Independence and happiness can't be demanded. Raising a son must be done so as to provide spaces into which he càn fit, and not the other way around.

My father died six weeks after my son was born. Dad had been sick on and off for some time. Many days he would be too scared or depressed to do much. When he did feel well, he overdid. The day that Michael was born, he and my mother came to see him. Dad couldn't make it to the hospital that day. He stayed at my house until my mother got back, and then they returned to Connecticut.

We named Michael after Marcie's father. The Jewish custom is to name a baby after someone recently departed, and Marcie's dad had died the year before. His middle name is Lawrence, after my dad. We brought him to Connecticut just a week or two before dad died. He had gone out and bought a onesie for him, with his large, rough hands.

Later, he tried to give him a bite of chocolate. Marcie and I stopped him, but he came through in true Larry fashion, growling, "What's the matter? The kid'll be fine. He likes it." The kid is fine. Both of the kids are fine. All of us are fine.

Thanks, Dad.

Chutes and Ladders

One Christmas, I got Chutes and Ladders, my first board game. I guess I was seven or eight at the time; I don't really remember. But I do remember how pleased I was when I figured out how to play it. There's a joy in mastery, a kind of affirmation that things are supposed to make sense, and you can make them do it.

I sat by myself, spinning the arrow and moving forward the requisite number of spaces. The real kick came when I hit one of the ladders. I'd put my game piece at the bottom rung and make a kind of swooshy noise as I slid it upward, passing all those boring single spaces. It was top-of-the-world time, baby, top of the world, until…

If you've ever played Chutes and Ladders, you'll remember the huge chute that slides down the center of the board. It's a tragic and dizzying plunge. One minute you're trotting blissfully to the winner's circle, and the next, calamity. My first reaction was to recount my steps. Surely there was some mistake. I'd done nothing to deserve this. I'd followed the rules, flicked the spinner with earnestness and hope, and now this. Of course there had to be a mistake. No soap. The count was correct.

I was enraged and humiliated. I hated the game, and whoever had given it to me. Why me? Why was I chosen to have this happen?

Now, you might wonder why I didn't just spin again. I was playing by myself. There was no one to object, no reason to take this beating, but that wouldn't heal the wound. For a rule follower like me, the real injury was that even when I was on my best behavior, something bad could happen. It was a matter of injustice. Play by the rules and everything will work out in the end. Well, this was the end. I wasn't ever going to play ever again, ever!

Well, you probably know how that goes for a seven- or eight-year-old. In a little while, some cousin or neighbor or someone wanted to play with my game, and I suddenly remembered the pride of ownership and the taste of mastery. Here was someone who didn't know the subtle and arcane strategies, someone I could teach—and surely beat. Out came the board, round went the spinner, up went the pieces, until my opponent hit the first little chute. Well, here was vindication. My earlier slide had been a fluke, an aberration. I had been meant to win, and now here it was.

I have to confess that I'm a bad loser, but a much worse winner. I'm willing to bet that no small amount of gloating was seen in that moment. Then a peaceful learning experience evolved into grim death. Snarls and tears quickly ended when my mother made us put the game away. I didn't like being punished, but I could see the logic in it. In a peculiar way, my predictable universe had been restored.

I am just beginning to see how much wisdom there is in Chutes and Ladders. We are given the gift of living, and sometimes we can see the cosmos in the way it works. We play with something we're not supposed to, we break it, and we get sent to time-out.

Or we make our mom a card for her birthday, and she tells us how great it is, and it gets put on the refrigerator as proof. That's how we'd like it to be, and it can be that way just enough for us to forget that chaos also has a role. You don't have to deserve to land on the bottom of a ladder—or the top of a chute. Deserving isn't always a factor.

In fact, I'm just old enough to be able to look back and see that life is chutes and ladders. It's good to learn the rules. It makes the game comprehensible. Knowing the right ways to do things gives us the best chance to have the outcomes that we want or have earned. But knowing the right ways to do things doesn't guarantee them.

Life has periods during which things are predictable and smooth. Days, weeks, months, and years pass, and we can explain every up and down that comes our way. Work hard, save your money, and you can retire early. Yeah, and then your lousy, lazy brother-in-law splits a hundred-million-dollar lottery ticket with a guy he met at a bar after his anger management class. You spin and move to the next space, he hits the ladder.

Then some poor high school kid who has never done a really dumb thing in her life has two drinks and gets behind the wheel of a car. You know the rest. Where's the justice in that?

What's the answer? For some it's the belief that the next life is where all bets are paid, where the final tally is taken. They may be right; I don't know. Most of us have times when the unfair breaks have us ready to tip over the game board and never play again. It's funny that the good luck seems to be some kind of payback, but truth be told, it's no more our due than the bad. I'm thinking that it's just life.

I'm tired enough to want to just ride out the storms and go fishing when the sun shines. I can't pretend that that's the answer, but I am pretty convinced that there's no future in spending a lot of time worrying about the question.

Your spin.

Breakfast

I went to Enfield Street School for first through third grades. That wasn't my parents' first plan. They wanted me to go to St. Joseph's Parochial School. I don't remember hearing them talk about it, but I do remember my father taking me to the rectory one Sunday to sign me up.

Now, my father's family, the D'Aleos, were a known quantity in the village of Thompsonville and the St. Patrick's Parish. It was typical of immigrant Italian families at that time. My father had three brothers and five sisters, all but one of whom lived in town—a respectable brood. Also in typical immigrant Italian style, all were Catholic, with the majority of the inevitable religious needs taken care of by the girls. My aunts dutifully brought Easter cakes to the sisters, made novenas whenever someone was sick, sewed curtains for the priests, and generally saw to it that god was aware of the good deeds they were doing.

My mother, being a convert and an Irish one at that, was suspect among the sisters, but being quiet and pretty, she was a hit among the brothers. This made things even worse. She was rarely included in most of the girl talk (which they conducted in Sicilian) and couldn't cook the way that they felt was proper.

Another strike against her was that my grandfather thought she was terrific. He liked looking at her and didn't mind at all that she wasn't Italian. She was quiet, kissed him on the cheek when she saw him, and made a grandson who was named after him. His attention and approval was the kiss of death to the sisters. Be clear, they would not ever defy him in any way to his face. He was the patriarch after all. It was their duty to obey, but they didn't have to approve.

Anyway, the D'Aleos were firmly established in the parish as a proper family. (All except for my father.) Right about the time I was ready for elementary school, the new priest, Father Direnzi, decided it was time to take things into the twentieth century. He was one of those righteous men of God who felt that their sacrifice entitled them to all the perks available. Among those was the use of an Oldsmobile, thick cigars, and oversight over the actions of all the members of his flock—and of course, free curtains. To keep track of the devotion of each of his charges, he instituted a practice called "using the envelopes" during the offering.

Everyone I knew went to mass every Sunday and every "holy day of obligation." Going to mass had a strict protocol, a set of rules probably established in Genesis. We had specific clothes just for that hour on Sunday, went to the same mass, sat in or near the same pew every week, and were expected to be able to endure indecipherable Latin for about an hour without fidgeting.

I have to digress here to say that for a five-year-old, the sixty minutes spent in church is equal to two and a half years to an adult. When you're sitting, you want to stand up. When you stand up, you can't see what's going on because everyone else is standing too, and they're all taller than you. The natural impulse is to step up on the kneeler to gain the extra six inches that affords, but that counts as a major fidget and earns an immediate stage-whispered threat from your mother. Kneeling can be mildly interesting if you can sneak a glance under the pew. Once I found a quarter doing that, which was a small fortune equal to a week's allowance.

Things got a little better after my First Communion, when I got my own missal. Although I never really understood how it was organized, it was something to read and therefore an improvement. The big plus came after a year or so, when I found the list of prayers and their associated indulgences in the back of the book. The good sisters at catechism let us know that we would almost assuredly be spending several millennia in purgatory, making up for the sins we were relentlessly committing every minute. The missal had prayers and the number of years you got off your sentence each time you said particular ones.

It became an enormous incentive to learn unit pricing. In that weekly hour I learned to count the syllables in every prayer, divide by the number of years off of purgatory, and ultimately discover which prayers gave the most "bang for the buck." Once that was established, I memorized them and repeatedly said them over and over throughout the hour. Given that god is omnipotent, I knew that he could make out the blurred vowels and consonants I blasted through. In just a few weeks, I could clean up to eight centuries of fire and brimstone in one mass.

Anyway, there was a protocol to mass, and one of the most prominent parts of it was the collection. At St. Pat's, ushers passed down the rows of pews, slipping long-handled baskets in front of the parishioners who seriously dropped in dimes, quarters, and halves. Once in a while, someone gave a dollar bill, but I thought that constituted grandstanding and god would see through it. Besides, anyone willing to give up a dollar must have had some big-time sins to make up for. For my part, I gave a dime. Each and every week, my dad would give me a dime to put into the basket. I never noticed what he was giving. It was this part of the process that changed the course of my education.

Father Direnzi's idea was to issue envelopes to every family in the parish. They came in a neat stack, each labeled with the name of the donor and the date of the offering. There was also a space to write the amount that was inside. My aunts thought this idea was perfect. Now god could know how devoted you were, with no chance of losing track. To my father, the idea was so absurd he couldn't take it seriously. Clearly a storm was on the horizon.

One Sunday after mass, instead of going home to create some new havoc in the basement, my dad walked me to the rectory. He knocked on the door. After a minute, Father Direnzi opened it and invited us in. His collar was loose. He had just put in his most critical work hour of the week and was lighting up his first cigar of the Sabbath. "What can I do for you?" he asked.

"I'm Larry D'Aleo. This is my son. I want to enroll him in St. Joe's."

"Larry D'Aleo? Larry D'Aleo? Oh, you're the D'Aleo who isn't using the envelopes."

Even at five, with no clue what they were talking about, I could tell a fuse was lit. "Yeah, and I'm the D'Aleo whose kid goes to public school." And we walked out. That was the last time my father went to mass without someone dying or getting married to get him there.

Now, public school wasn't a bad place. Since I already could read, and my math skills had been honed in the house of the lord, the work was no problem. I rolled through Dick and Jane without effort or reward. I never heard of a family that was so boring. While the rank and file was counting to twenty, I could watch the lovely Linda Morris, with her chestnut hair, and long for something mysterious but enticing. I played well with most others most of the time, so I thought I had it made.

Then came my first Friday. Friday was hot lunch day, with an unremarkable (and mostly unrecognizable) menu. A bored lunch lady put a plate on my tray. Maybe fish sticks, possibly mashed potatoes from a mix, and most emphatically peas. Peas. Good lord! Peas! They put them on every plate. Just walking to my spot at the table had me retching. It was my first cold sweat. Peas! Holy crap! What was I going to do?!

My family had some odd ideas about eating, ideas that had been formed during the Depression. Anything put in front of you had to be eaten. There was a corollary to this rule, which could be summarized as the more you hate a food item, the better it is for you. According to this, peas were the best possible thing anyone could ever eat. I learned at home that there could be no deviation from this rule. I had the peas, and I was expected to eat them.

Then came the miracle. Miss Schultz, the third-grade goddess/ teacher saw me, pale and sweating. She came over from her seat and asked me if I felt all right. As a matter of fact, I didn't, but it never occurred to me that that would be a relevant factor in my situation. Nature gives humans very few instincts, but survival is one. Without thinking, I shook my head in a pathetic no, using the perfect angle to illicit sympathy. I had no idea what might happen if I did this, but some primitive drive led me to act. Miss Schultz let out with a coo of support, took me by the hand, and walked me away from the offending legumes. Where we were going did not matter at all. I was being led by the most beautiful woman in the world other than my mother, and not just led, but taken away from peas.

I had only been in school for a week, so I wasn't aware of the nurse's office, but that's where we went. The nurse couldn't touch Miss Schultz for beauty, but she had a cot, a kind manner, and no peas. My time telling was a little shaky, but I knew that lunch was only twenty minutes, and ten of them had already passed. If I could hold out just a little longer, the green death would lose its power over me.

The nurse quickly found that I didn't have a temperature, wasn't bleeding, and could identify no specific malady. I lay down on the cot for a while, and then she asked me how I was feeling. Much better was my answer. Lunch was over, and recess was looming. As I returned to class, I was reminded of the ticker-tape parades that greeted our GIs after World War II. I had faced the enemy and won overwhelmingly.

As an adult, I can see that my triumph was fatally flawed, but at five I thought I had it knocked. My confidence lasted until the next Friday. My main defense was a gift for retching with almost no prompting, and just knowing that a pea was in the same state was more than enough to start my gagging.

The first scenario seemed to be repeating itself. My guardian angel recognized my distress and brought me to the nurse. She took my temperature and left me relaxing on the cot. But then it all came crashing down—the nurse called my mom. It took Mom about two minutes to come walking into the office. What she saw was me lounging on the cot, waiting for the bell to start recess.

My reverie screeched to a halt when I heard her voice. I was too naïve to know what I was doing wrong, but when she walked in, I was confident that I would soon find out. Nurse talks to mom. Mom talks to nurse. Mom and nurse look at me. Mom comes over and puts her hand on my forehead. No temperature. "Hmmm? Did you eat?"

"No, there were peas..."

"Peas?"

"Yeah, green ones."

To the nurse: "You said this happened last week too, were there peas last week too?"

"Well, yes, we have peas every Friday."

Mystery disease diagnosed. Cure: bagged lunch on Fridays. The only downside was it meant an interruption in my visits with the lovely Miss Schultz.

Some school issues are harder to solve, especially when they run counter to family values. In my family, saving money was big. We weren't exactly needy, but my parents knew what needy felt like, and lived as if we were. I was five and had no clue one way or another, except for my pants.

To save money, my mother was making my pants, and about pants I was particular. Perhaps that's a little deceptive. Ordinary pants were fine with me, but my mother was making my pants out of wool. She cut them out with care, using the best wool she could find. She lined them with flannel and stitched them precisely. After all, my pants were a reflection of her skills as a mother, so they needed to be perfect. To me, it wouldn't have mattered if she's lined them with titanium—the wool itched.

Nothing is more miserable than an itchy six-year-old. Once it starts, there's no solution. Scratching is useless. No cream, ointment, or magic potion can relieve it. It just has free rein until it decides to stop on its own. I can testify from experience that this is true.

It started innocently enough. How was I to know that I would be wearing woolen pants? I was six, and if my mom didn't dress me, I'd go around naked. The whole issue didn't emerge until the weather got cold. I believe my mother was just waiting for a chance to show how well she took care of her kid.

Near the end of November, just after my birthday, we had our first frost. Out came the pants from wherever they'd been kept. By all normal standards, they should have been harmless, but in less than five minutes, it started.

"These itch me."

"These *what* itch you?"

"These pants itch me."

Mom's first response was psychological. "Okay, let me fix them." Off they came. She looked them over intently, shook them out, smoothed them with her hands, and put them back on me. "That ought to do it."

"They still itch me."

Frustration levels being what they are, and reality being counter to the possibility of really itching with the flannel lining, Mom said "No, they can't itch you."

"Well, they do."

"Don't"

"Do too."

"Don't."

Now I began to sense danger. Mom could be pushed only so far, and we were getting close. She'd spent a long time making those pants. Maybe I should reconsider whether or not I was really itching. Don't get me wrong. I didn't have a handle on the idea of placebo itching, but I was willing to reexamine my perceptions in the interest of keeping the peace.

Off to school we went, Mom driving with clenched jaw, silently daring me to say a word. With trepidation and growing thigh irritation, I shuffled into the building.

The next six hours were torture. I tried every kind of walking imaginable, finally settling on a sort of bow-legged hop-shuffle that would get me access to handicapped parking if I did it today. Recess, normally remarkable for iron-clad diversions like throwing pinecones at girls and pretending to be the Lone Ranger, was spent trying to keep the cloth from touching my legs. Sitting at my desk was more of an attempt to hover over the seat to keep the wool from contacting my butt.

Today I realize that the wool could absolutely not touch my legs. The lining should have been foolproof, but by day's end, my inner thighs were a dull rosy color that would be very nice on a bathroom wall, but was just ugly on a six-year-old. As soon as I got home, it was obvious that something was up. There was no conversation, no recrimination.

That weekend, we took a special trip to J.C. Penney's. Mom bought me two pairs of chino pants and one of corduroy. We never spoke of it again.

An Optimal Learning Environment

As a teacher, I do my best to create a classroom in which students can master skills and concepts. I strive to help them build self-esteem, so that they can enter the world with confidence and competence. I do this because I'm old enough to know what kids need as adults. Anyway, that's my story, and I'm sticking to it, but it most certainly didn't seem that way at Enfield Street School when I was a kid.

When I was a first-grader, it was all about recess. The playground was where it all happened, where we heard dirty words our parents didn't use, experienced triumph and tragedy at Red Rover, and got the first hints that girls might be different from boys. Teachers' unions being what they were, there was never more than one teacher for every three hundred kids; so, unless you could show a protruding bone, you were left to your own devices.

Essentially, we had to rely on our imaginations to sustain us. What were schools thinking? Some days, I was a wild pony, galloping across the hardtop, passing just close enough to the fourth-grade girls to be annoying, but far enough away to avoid them noticing. Other days, my friend Herbert and I would spy on Eddie Lavangie and his friend Jay, hiding in plain sight from each other for no reason any of us could name.

Our games rarely lasted more than a day or two, before something else would capture our fantasies. But some days are just different from the rest. On those days, things change and don't change back for a long time. The Kennedy assassination was like that, as was the moon landing. Not all these special days affect the whole world. The Day of the Killer Robot was like that.

To understand the Day of the Killer Robot, you have to have some idea of the geography of my grade school. Enfield Street School was, not surprisingly, on Enfield Street. The street is one of those wide New England roads that you could put on a postcard. It has antique houses with gracious lawns and mature maple trees. The school is right across from the church where the colonists were alerted to the invading British. It's also right behind the Old Town Hall, which is central to the story.

In the mid-1950s, when I spent my recesses on the playground, the Old Town Hall had been out of use and neglected for years. It was once a handsome building, with classic Greek Revival columns and perfect triangular pediments. Now it had boarded-up windows and peeling paint. The chain-link fence that defined the schoolyard also abutted the back of the Old Town Hall. I had never noticed it. I knew it was there, but it had no impact on my life. Then came the Day of the Killer Robot.

It's impossible to tell how it all started. It seemed like any other day at recess. Herbert and I were warming to our ongoing debate—Roy Rogers versus the Lone Ranger—when suddenly everyone was running toward the fence. When everyone else on a playground runs somewhere, you run too. So Herbert and I raced there.

An impossible crush against the fence ensued. Clearly panic was the order of the day, but the reason for it was as yet unclear. All at once, there was a parting of the crowd, as Miss Rossini, my ancient first-grade teacher stalked up. She was on playground duty, but in no mood to play. Her face had clotted red when everyone left the blacktop to go to the fence. This was as forbidden as it would have been in a prison, but what could she do? Every kid in the school had done it.

As she came up, a breathless and smarmy sixth-grade girl rushed over to her and said "Miss Rossini, there's a robot in the Old Town Hall! Raymond O'Neil saw it in the window." Half a century later, I realize that my fellow student Raymond O'Neil was born to sell used cars. The only time he was lying was when his lips were moving. Even as a six-year-old, I could sense that Raymond O'Neil was probably someone to avoid, but for some reason, his report of a robot was unquestioned. That is, unquestioned until Miss Rossini entered the frame.

Raymond was relatively easy to pick out of the throng. He was expounding authoritatively on the vision at the window, his description remarkably similar to a robot recently seen on the screen at the Strand Theatre on Pearl Street. Eventually, I'm sure Raymond would become a senator or maybe have a political talk show on cable, but on this day, he was no match for the raging Rossini. The bell rang before his fate could be revealed to me. I did see his father go into the principal's office, but that wasn't particularly unusual. He visited the principal at least once a week.

When we were safely back in our classrooms, the issue seemed dead. It was silly to believe Raymond. What would a robot be doing in the Old Town Hall? How could it be seen in a window when the windows were boarded up? In a while, the excitement was forgotten, replaced by a new Dr. Seuss tour de force in the reading corner.

But killer robots don't go away easily. It all came back to me just after I put my coat on while waiting for the dismissal bell. What if Raymond wasn't lying? Why would he lie about something as solemn as that? Maybe the robot peeked out the door, and not the window? Anyone could misspeak under circumstances like that. As for why a killer robot would be in the Old Town Hall, the obvious rejoinder is why not? It was just the kind of abandoned building where I would put one if I had one. Suddenly I wasn't so eager for the dismissal bell.

I was a walker. I lived just about a mile from the school, but with no major streets to cross and no daily reports of terrorists waiting around every corner, I was expected to make the trip alone. For the first day or two, my mother walked with me, just to make sure I knew the way. It wasn't hard. To the end of my street, take a right and in fifteen minutes I was there. I actually enjoyed that part of my day. There were always interesting sticks to pick up; planes landing across the river at Bradley Field were good for a distraction; and once I found a robin's eggshell.

All that happened before a killer robot moved into the neighborhood. The main thing to worry about was walking in front of the Old Town Hall itself. That was right in the beginning of my walk, but it wasn't the end of the trouble. Killer robots were known to play with their victims, letting them think that the danger had passed before closing in for the kill. Because the large majority of my walk was with my back to the threat, I was a mess.

Mom was more than a little surprised when I breathlessly crashed through the screen door in record time. The crashing part wasn't particularly surprising—I did that every day—but today I was early. Not just a little early—*really* early. No six-year-old had ever before covered a mile in five minutes. She wanted to know why.

There isn't a kid in the world who doesn't know the rule. Boys from Sri Lanka to Managua know that if you talk about a killer robot, that makes it more real. I was born knowing that, but I also knew that my mother wasn't going to settle for "I dunno." I was trapped.

I started with a classic stammer, followed by the always serviceable lower-lip quiver. Struggling for control, I began to gasp for breath. The pressure was mounting by the second. I couldn't talk and I couldn't stay silent. I crumbled in short order, and it all came out in a rush. My mother did her best not to laugh as I gasped out the story. I knew she was taking it seriously though, because she said, "Wait until your father hears this!"

Generally, it was considered wise to tell my father nothing. There was rarely a way to predict how he might react to things, but my mother seemed positive that he had to know about this. As I thought about it myself, I began to warm to the idea. You see, my dad was the biggest man who ever lived. He was at least nine feet tall, with muscles like Tarzan. When he blew his nose, the earth shook. The president of the world used to call him up to get advice about how the handle those pesky Ruskies. Yeah, my dad was just the man for this killer robot situation. Settled into the idea that he would soon be on the case, I relaxed enough to eat a snack and watch a little television.

At five o'clock, my father got home. He had spent another day building airplanes at Hamilton Standard and was anxious to unwind. I stayed where I was, while he and Mom talked in the kitchen. I was anticipating conspiratorial whisperings, serious discussion, followed by a firm plan of action that included airstrikes and loud shouting. What I got was laughter, soft chuckling at first, but building steadily to an undignified braying that was almost insulting. Where could this lead?

At dinner, my father asked me how school was. How was school? *How was school?!* What did that matter when I was dealing with a cold, mechanical killer? "Mom told me about Raymond and the robot." Now we were getting somewhere. "When I was your age, we didn't worry about robots."

This wasn't news to me—he was as big as a mountain, robots worried about him. "When I was your age, we worried about gorillas." Gorillas? Huh? What was he talking about? "Yeah, there was a movie about a gorilla that everyone saw, and for a month afterward, I was sure there was one in our cellar. Now, Raymond is a jerk. (Dad didn't hesitate to call a spade a spade.) There is no robot. Not in the Old Town Hall, not in the church across the street, not anywhere. There is no robot. That's for sure."

Well, he was my dad, and he would know. But this didn't end all my anxiety. I remained uneasy about walking in front of the Old Town Hall for years afterward, but the worst was over. At least the worst about killer robots. I did begin to have nightmares about gorillas in the basement.

Sixty-One

I remember the summer Roger Maris hit sixty-one home runs. I was ten going on eleven. The neighborhood kids and I spent every day playing some form of baseball, all the while listening to Yankees games on our new portable radios. By "some form of baseball," I mean sandlot games with four kids to a side, or a whiffle ball and bat in someone's backyard, or "bounder and a fly" in the street, or anything involving some kind of ball and bat.

Summers were hotter then, but we minded less. Our mothers sent us out in the morning as soon as we got through with our Rice Krispies or Cheerios, and didn't expect to see us again until they bellowed for us through the screen door. The only exception was if the neighborhood kids happened to settle in your yard. Then Mom could count on a more or less steady stream of dirty kids using the bathroom or getting a drink of water. No one knocked on the door to do this. They just sprinted in, said, "Hi, Mrs. Whoever!" peed with the seat down or drank from the faucet, and sprinted out again.

These trips would be cut in half as soon as the garden hose was hooked up. The water was invariably just past lukewarm, with a unique rubbery taste that I remember to this day. Drinking from a garden hose is probably the cause of a thousand diseases from which we suffer now, but who could have known that then. We weren't totally out of touch with some possible health troubles that could result. No one I knew ever drank without first letting the water run long enough to wash out the spiders that we were sure lurked just inside the opening.

I'm not sure why we knew this. I imagine that someone had a cousin who knew a kid somewhere who accidentally swallowed a daddy-long-legs, and so we were judicious about washing them out before drinking. I'm certain no one knew the fate of the spider swallower; it wasn't necessary for any details to be revealed. We all knew that nothing could be worse than that.

Anyway, that summer was remarkable for Mantle and Maris, hitting homers at a rate not seen since Babe Ruth's days. We knew all the Yankees on the team, and most of us had particular favorites. Yogi Berra, Whitey Ford, Bobby Richardson, Clete Boyer—each one was someone's hero, but Mantle and Maris caught everyone's imagination.

Mantle was everything any of us wanted to be. A great hitter, he ran with speed and grace, making impossible catches in the outfield look easy. He had the proverbial cannon for an arm, and his hitting... well, the easiest way to get a good fistfight going was the Ted Williams/ Mickey Mantle "who was the better hitter" controversy.

It's worth a moment here to explain that I grew up on the most volatile border in the world: north central Connecticut. The next town north of us was Longmeadow, Massachusetts, the beginning of Red Sox country. We were the last geographical bastion of the Yankee nation, so we bore the enormous responsibility of defending the Yanks from the degenerate, mistaken Red Sox followers. This border still exists. And I'm proud to say that my contribution to the good fight has helped defend it from the encroachment of rational thinking about overpaid, mercenary athletes.

Roger Maris was different. I don't remember him being particularly noteworthy before or after that summer. For most of the season, it was unclear which one of them would end up with more homers. It seesawed back and forth, game by game, as we scuffed up our Converse sneakers in vacant lots and backyards. There were always at least three transistor radios tuned to the same station on day games. Endless pitches, "burned in" and argued over, were punctuated by Mantle/Maris at-bats, when we all stopped playing and hovered over the nearest radio until the transcendent moment was over, one way or the other.

Home runs weren't the only memorable events, of course. There was the time our fellow player, Jimmy Antonio, was hit in the groin by a line drive. It was the first time that particular catastrophe befell any of us, and it was with clinical precision that we all stood over him as he rolled around in the dirt, clutching the afflicted area, making fascinating sounds that were somewhere between gurgles and whimpers. Someone thought to get Jimmy's sixteen-year-old brother (not someone known for either his gentle manner or affection for his kid brother), but a good alternative to his mother, who could never be told of this calamity. As it was, Jimmy's brother was grateful for the opportunity to observe this historic moment. When he caught his breath from laughing, he offered the standard medical advice. "Walk it off."

The summer was also remarkable for the day I caught two line drives in the field beside St. Joseph's School. I was a year younger than nearly every kid in the neighborhood, so it was almost universally accepted that I was hopelessly incapable of any athletic endeavor. I faced and accepted the fact that I would always be chosen last for any game in which Mikey Andrews didn't play.

Mikey was the only kid younger than me. He was allowed to play for two reasons. First, he was willing to go under the fence at St. Joe's to retrieve foul balls hit in the scrub brush beside the railroad tracks, and second, because his tomboy sister Ellen played with us every game and would beat the crap out of anyone but Dave Anderson if Mikey was excluded.

Dave Anderson was my hero. He was actually everyone's hero. He was one of those boys who was good at everything they put their mind to. He was an exceptional athlete, did well enough in school to keep the nuns off his back, but not so well that he was unlikeable by the rank and file. He had enthusiasm without being unseemly and was inherently kind to everyone.

Anyway, back to the game. For some reason, I was put in left field, where I was expected to lean against the chain link fence, pick up any ball that rolled that far, and throw it at someone else on my team, who would relay it to whichever base was relevant at the time. The first half of the miracle happened early. Jimmy hit a ball hard toward left. I was daydreaming, as was my wont, so the crack of the bat had little impact on my reveries. What did bring me around was Dave's holler "Get it!" Suddenly I saw it coming right toward me.

Time slowed down as I flashed on Mickey Mantle. No loping dive was needed as I held my glove open. Jimmy's "screamer" lasered right in. The field was silent. I'd never caught anything before. Jimmy was furious. Any ball hit in my direction was generally considered at least a ground rule double, but there could be no controversy here. The ball was clearly caught, and Jimmy was out.

The second liner, a statistical miracle, came in the last inning. It was perhaps more mundane than the first, once again beginning with my spacing out in left field. The catch itself was a tribute to the sympathetic nervous system, occurring because I happened to glance down from a particularly interesting cloud shaped like a fish, just as the ball closed in on my head. The glove went up, the ball went in, end of story.

This time, the crowd wasn't stunned; rather, I sensed their disappointment. I guess they'd hoped for some kind of repeat of the Jimmy groin experience, but my glove dashed that hope. I felt no rancor about this, I understood their disappointment completely.

Anyway, '61 was a singularly special summer. I've probably lumped all the summers of my youth into that package of memories, but so what? Maris hit the most runs, Mantle had a stellar year, the Yankees won the Series, and all was as it should have been. These days, summer is filled with Japanese beetle grubs and leaks in the pool lining.

Community Standards

I grew up in a very diverse community. There were Irish Catholics and Italian Catholics. They worshipped at St. Patrick's, where my parents were married and where I received all the sacraments I've gotten so far. There were Polish Catholics, who worshipped at St. Adelbert's, mostly under a legend known as Father Paul. The Polish community lived and died by his pronouncements. No one could chew more cigars, eat more pierogi, or spit farther than Father Paul.

In addition to Catholics, on the other side of town, in the section named Hazardville (so called after a Civil War gunpowder manufacturer named Colonel Augustus Hazard), there were plenty of rock-ribbed Yankee Protestant tobacco farmers. This was a lucky and exotic tribe by my reckoning, because they didn't bother with church on Sunday. I thought that this pretty much ruled out a pleasant afterlife for them, but Sundays were their own.

In high school, my world really opened up. I met a Jew. I didn't know he was a Jew right off. People didn't go around advertising these things. I found out through a series of deductions. First, his last name ended in "ski," but he didn't go to the Polish church. Next, he and his sister shared a Pontiac GTO that their parents bought for them. And finally, their father was a doctor. Taken by themselves, these facts would have been curious, but as a trio, the conclusion was unmistakable. Anyway, by the time I found out about his Jewishness, he had already entered my social circle.

In this melting pot, my father taught me a kind of universal view of all mankind. It could be summed up as "Everyone you haven't known for at least ten years is out to screw you. In addition, many of those you have known for at least ten years are also out to screw you, but you know them, so it should be harder for them to do it." Curiously, there wasn't a single element of stereotyping involved in any of this. They weren't untrustworthy because of their race, ethnicity, sex, age, or whatever. They were untrustworthy because they were human, and humans mostly just couldn't help it.

When I was young, he taught these lessons through a lifetime of stories and examples, drawn from his experiences. "That nice Uncle Antonio you like so much took my rabbit in 1927, and I haven't seen it since. During the Depression, we shoveled the school parking lot together. The principal paid us a nickel, and he kept the three cents."

As I grew older, my father was eager to assist me in examining my own experiences. He must have worshipped me, his oldest son, because he usually called me Jesus Christ. "Jesus Christ, you traded a baseball to Donnie for a Ted Williams baseball card? A pack of cards costs five cents; a baseball is a dollar. Jesus Christ, are you crazy?"

The thread that ran through all of these moments (and it felt like they happened every day) was that the world was a dangerous place. People were not to be trusted with anything of value. Watch your back at all times. These were lessons he learned while raising two younger brothers pretty much on his own. His youngest sister needed treatment for polio, and his mother took six of the kids with her. Someone, though, had to drop out of school to help take care of the other two while my grandfather did whatever a Sicilian man who owned more than one dress shirt did.

Dad was fifteen, and had little patience for what they taught in school anyway. He claimed he learned all he needed to know in first grade; they taught him to read. So he stopped going to school and ran the family grocery. He learned to be disappointed in people, to be absolutely loyal to friends, and to avoid showing his loved ones feelings other than anger. After all, this was the kind of territorial dominance display that kept the predators at bay. He didn't learn or teach prejudice.

Before my second marriage, my fiancée, Marcie, and I were terrified to introduce her mother to my father. He was an eighth-grade drop-out; she had two PhDs and a master's degree. He was an iconoclastic Catholic who went to church only for funerals, and she taught Jewish conversion classes. My father was a lover of stone masonry and geometry; she believed in art and music. The day looked to be a remake of King Kong meets Godzilla.

But our worry was in vain, because as always, he rose to meet a real challenge with much more grace than one would have imagined. He told her a story. It seems when his mother was in New York, he would spend a week or two with her in the summers. He was streetwise enough to get along, and even made a few friends in the neighborhood. Among these was a Jewish kid, with whom he went home for a couple of minutes to pick up something or other.

What he saw in this kid's home was the boy's mother feeding her baby honey from the cover of a book. Ever generous, he was touched. He knew what it felt like to need things, but his family at least had plates. The next day, he scrounged up a couple of dishes and brought them over.

The mother was taken aback, not remembering the scene when he'd visited before. She thanked him for the gift, but followed with the question of why he'd brought it. He stammered that his family had more than they needed and that the baby ought to have a dish. The story ended with the mother smiling. She told my father that he could take back the dishes. They had plenty. She just wanted her baby to associate books with the sweeter things in life.

With that story, a covenant was sealed between my father and my future mother-in-law.

What can we take from all this? The world can indeed be a treacherous place. People are not to be trusted, but not to be trusted with what? You can trust a stranger who asks for a quarter to spend it on something. He might spend it on drink, or he might need it for a hot meal. We don't really know which for sure, but we know that if we have enough to spare, we can leave it up to the person who's asking to decide what to do with our generosity.

We're not fools for trusting in this way. When we enter into any human transaction, we should know what we have to lose and what we have to spare. That is critical. Trust others with what we have to spare, and we've done our duty. Irish Catholics, Italian Catholics, Polish Catholics, Protestants, Jews, Druids, Elves, and anyone else should be able to get into heaven doing that.

Currier and Ives

Thompsonville was a small town when I was growing up. It had a firehouse, a J.C. Penny's, a mill pond, and churches around its center. There was an appliance store, a store for buying shoes, and even a store where a man sat and rolled cigars in the window. The shoe store was one of our favorites because it had a machine that allowed us to X-ray our feet for a penny. It looked like one of those bathroom scales that had a high post in the middle that stood up to let the nearsighted among us read our weight. But this machine let us actually see the bones in our feet.

I'm sure we were all getting horrible diseases from this, but at the time no one thought about things in those terms. Our mothers were just glad that we were occupied long enough for them to try on shoes or get us fitted for our summer Chuck Taylors in peace.

The town center was built around the Bigelow Sanford Carpet Factory, which sat for more than a century beside the railroad tracks and the Connecticut River. It was the main industry in town in its day, and most old-timers worked there at one time or another. I'm proud to say that I worked there the summer before I went to college. I learned more there in that summer than I learned in many years of school.

There was the Thompsonville Hotel next door to it, where bachelors lived, with a barber shop in the basement that I heard once held a pool table for the idlers. There was the Strand Theatre that showed double features and kiddie matinees on Saturdays and a bar and grill that was the site of some of my most pleasant childhood memories. The place was called Vic's after the owner, and it had a ladies' entrance, a mounted deer's head on one wall, and most wondrous of all, a dumb-waiter.

Until the time that my father opened his store in 1957, he and I went to Vic's nearly every Saturday. We'd walk in and a half a dozen men would call out to my father, "Hey, Skur!" and he'd return a greeting. (Skur was his nickname. I never found out where it came from.) He'd order a glass of beer and get a second small glass. He'd put an inch or so in it for me, and I'd wisely add just a pinch of salt to it.

My father wasn't a big drinker, and giving me a little of his beer wasn't thought of as unusual at the time. The men in the bar were the sons of immigrants, like my father. They'd drunk wine or beer with meals their whole lives. For me, it was an acknowledgement of my membership in the realm of manhood. This perception was bolstered by the warmth these men felt for my father. They called me Little Skur, and they laughed when, at four or five, I corrected Vic the bartender by telling him that "it's not polite to say ain't."

As in all small towns, everyone knew everyone else, and everyone knew who was "different." Thompsonville had three such people. I'm not proud to say that we called one Crazy Anna, another Crazy Roger, and the third the Hermit. Crazy Anna and Crazy Roger were mentally handicapped adults who roamed around the center of town. As I said, everyone knew them, and their routines were as much a part of the fabric of the community as the six o'clock whistle that went off every day at the factory. They harmed no one, and no one harmed them.

The Hermit was a different kind of different; he was a mad genius. It would be obvious to anyone who saw him that he was odd. He rode around the town on a bicycle that he powered with a mongrelized motor. He wore an outlandishly long coat, and he lived in a two-story, two-room shed that he'd built beside a stream from which he generated his own electricity. He talked to almost no one.

The Hermit was strange enough for even me to notice, and I asked my father about him. It seems that he hadn't always been a hermit. A long time before, he had lived on the grounds of a large estate nearby. He had developed some improvement to automobiles, but the owner of the estate stole the idea from him, patented it, became even richer than he'd been before, and sent the Hermit into self-imposed exile.

My father went on to tell me that the Hermit had tolerated my dad when he was young, because my father was very mechanically inclined himself, as well as having a firm footing in antisocial behavior. The Hermit was deaf, and Dad had offered to help him get a hearing aid. The Hermit refused, growling that he didn't want to hear what most people were saying anyway.

The Hermit was peculiar in other ways as well. He never had any money, so he ate at the pleasure of anyone willing to feed him. This most often was Vic. Vic had once given him a couple of dollars to help him out, and the Hermit took it across the center of town to a coffee shop and bought himself lunch. Vic was a little hurt. After all, he had his own restaurant. The Hermit regally told him that just because he'd taken his money, it didn't mean he had to eat his food.

This apparent ingratitude triggered an event that tickled my father as much as anything in many years. In the 1950s, Hamilton Standard and Pratt and Whitney Aircraft had booming factories running across the river from Thompsonville, and many men, including my father, worked there. One of the regulars at Vic's was a machinist at Hamilton—one of those men who was bothered by everything and who took most of his pleasure in complaining.

He had access to the most sophisticated machinery in the world, and he decided to use it to put the ungrateful Hermit in his place. He took a common pin to work, and during his lunch break drilled a hole through its diameter. The next time the Hermit came into Vic's, the machinist sneered at him and said, "You're so smart, let's see you do something like this." He shoved the pin in the Hermit's face, put it on the bar, and puffed his chest out in triumph. The Hermit said nothing. He picked up the pin and left without whatever it was he'd come in for in the first place.

The next week or so passed without incident, save the machinist's ongoing smugness. Finally, one evening, the Hermit came into Vic's as usual. He cadged a meal and walked out the door. Immediately after, he turned around, went up to his tormenter, and handed him back his pin. "I almost forgot," he said "I fixed it." Upon close examination his meaning became clear. In his shack, he'd threaded the hole and made a screw to fit it.

Late in life, my father took to repairing clocks and watches. He was a member of various groups of ex-watchmakers and master craftsmen from all over the country, but he never saw anyone able to do what the Hermit did to shut someone up.

My wife, Marcie and I live in a small town. It's a lovely community, with very little crime, good schools, and excellent services. The lawns are well tended, and the schools always get the funding they need for whatever they ask. Our kids have been raised in this town. The education they've received has allowed them both to go to prestigious colleges.

Despite that, there are drawbacks to this kind of living. A stable community can easily become a rigid one. If you're a good tee-ball player at seven, you'll probably earn a spot on the high school varsity team when you're fifteen, but if you wet your pants in the second grade, god help you; that's who you'll always be.

Our town has clearly defined values and roles. If you fit into them easily, you can live your childhood out knowing that you are perfectly who everyone should be. There aren't many opportunities to doubt that our way is *the* way.

For my kids, getting out into the bigger world has been important. It fell to Marcie to foster this, because I didn't realize that our world was so small. Michael did theater in Boston, starting when he was nine. He was going into the city for months before he realized he was there. It shocked him to be in Boston, because he'd seen no shootings and robberies. As he spent more time there, he met kids who rode the subway, had to make their own breakfast because their parents left for work before they went to school, and didn't go to Disney World every year for winter vacation.

Julie always had some sort of instinct that the herd she encountered in town may not have the only set of answers for living. She was often friendly enough, but rarely interested enough in Coach handbags and Abercrombie and Fitch clothing to be in the crowd. These days, an interesting thing has happened to her. She's spent summers in Mexico and been away at college for a year. Now she has chosen to be more conscious of clothing and appearance. I think the key here is *chosen*. She has seen the options for ways to be, and she has accepted some for herself.

In a small town, it's a danger that some good options aren't present, leaving some kids to feel like outsiders, to feel different when different is bad. The sad part is that some of them never realize that they are perfect in some other context.

In the Good Ole Summertime

It's the dog days, high eighties and humid. These days bring me back to the summers of my youth. If you ask my kids about their summers, they might tell you about basketball or soccer camps, or they might talk about lifeguarding or nannying for spending money. That's what kids do these days, it seems. I was lucky enough to have had a different experience.

In Connecticut, where I grew up, there was a proscribed plan for summer. My father followed it, as did his father, and so on down the line. We had the good fortune to "work on tobacco." The Connecticut River Valley in northern Connecticut and southern Massachusetts has a long tradition of growing the tobacco that's used as wrappers in the making of fine cigars. There's something about the soil there that makes it ideal for the broad, juicy leaves. This tobacco is grown in two ways. Either its "shade" grown under acres of cheesecloth tents, or the young plants are clipped early, so that they grow bushy. This method is called broadleaf, and it's the less common type.

When kids in my area hit fourteen, they were eligible to work on a tobacco farm. Parents rejoiced that the summer was set and that their kids would begin to feel the rewards of hard work. The companies had a system in place that made it all pretty easy. You signed up I don't remember where, maybe the guidance office at the high school, and you were told which farm hired you and where to go to get picked up the first day.

Pick up for me was at the top of my hill, on the main road. A school bus came, just like it did for the rest of the year, only this time it came at around five-thirty in the morning. The driver was one of those schoolteachers who was always looking for a way to pick up a few extra bucks and who often was waiting for a better paying civil service job to open up. The bus filled up with bleary-eyed fourteen- and fifteen-year-olds, carrying lunches in paper bags and wearing cut-off jeans. No one talked because everyone was already tired. We just sat in our seats, feeling the day heat up like only July days heat up.

The bus would take us to a farmyard in Suffield, where a forty-year-old wearing a hat and a perpetual scowl would tell a twenty-year-old "straw boss" which field we'd be working that day. By this time, it was probably close to seven, and we'd pile back into the bus and ride a little more to some endless field covered by a white tent and bordered by fecund fencerows. They always smelled like I imagined a jungle to smell, both rich and threatening.

In the early morning, the fields were soaking with dew. At first, we could walk along the rows, dribbling dusty fertilizer from pails or "suckering" the immature plants. Because they were so young, you could see all the way across, sometimes for a couple of hundred yards. It was like being in an aircraft hangar, vast space under white netting.

Tobacco grows very quickly, and by the time each field was fertilized and suckered in turn, the plants were pushing bulges into the top. If a row was flat and straight, you could maybe see fifteen feet. Any further was a Charlton Heston jungle of green heat. Suckering was miserable, but picking was worse. Each field was picked a number of times, starting with the leaves on the bottom of each plant.

We worked in teams of three, one hauling a canvas basket through the middle of two pickers on their butts, scootching along, taking the three bottom leaves from every plant in the rows on either side of them. Four plants and twelve leaves were called a pad, and pads were placed on the ground where the hauler could load them into his basket. The basket had to be loaded in a careful pattern, so that the workers in the shed could take them out intact, stitch them over laths, and hang them to dry.

Hauling was easy at the beginning of the row, but got progressively harder as the pickers got further and further from the end of the field. Eventually, they'd be sprinting through the filthy heat, "encouraged" by the straw boss, who had no one else in his life to bear the burden of his dissatisfaction.

The fields were measured in a unit called "bents." You could keep track of them, because a bent was the distance between the poles that held up the nets. As I recall, it was about ten yards. Some fields were twenty bents or more long. After a couple of weeks, we knew and especially dreaded the longer fields, and we knew and just hated the shorter ones. Pick followed pick, and we went from butt to knees and from knees to a miserable squat, always picking the bottom three leaves, always running to fill those baskets.

Tobacco is a consistent plant. It's dirty, itchy, and awful from start to finish. Its sole use, as far as I know, is to addict humans to its burning, and it gives hideous diseases for doing so. When you work with its plants, you quickly get covered in a sticky sap that attracts and holds dirt in a marvelous grip. It builds up into a layer an eighth of an inch thick on your skin that soap can't touch. We used brass brushes to remove the bulk of it, and only the first two weeks of school could remove the rest.

We eventually began to take revenge on the plants. The straw bosses knew that the plants were more important than any of us, and they made sure we didn't damage them. Carelessness that injured one of them got you chewed out in a way that only lifetime farmers can do, but we learned to get around that. For all its size and quick growth, tobacco has a fatal frailty. Underneath its thick stock, it has a tender, brittle core. If you grip its two-inch stock near the base and twist, that core breaks. You can feel it, and almost hear it snap. It doesn't show on the outside, and the plant doesn't seem any less robust; but in a couple of days, it's dead.

We were never there to see our own handiwork. No field was big enough to keep us there for that long, but as we picked our own rows, we would come across plants that others had assassinated previously. The discovery gave us a little thrill, a feeling of brotherhood with the other filthy, exhausted teens who rode the bus with us each morning.

Payday was magical. On Friday, the big boss would drive up in an almost super-natural Oldsmobile. He'd get out and hitch up his pants while the straw boss would slither over to fawn. The checks would be in the boss's back pocket. He'd stretch for a second, take off his hat to wipe off the sweat, and talk about how poorly the workers were, how much more quickly things needed to be going, and so on. It was the age-old process of misery rolling downhill. We knew the straw boss would vent his misery on us, but on Friday it didn't matter.

Eventually, after the proper amount of tantalizing, the boss would call us over to the bus, and as we got on for the ride home, we'd get our checks. The year I was fifteen, minimum wage for farm work was $1.05 an hour. Believe it or not, $1.05 was a princely sum then. After deductions, we took home nearly thirty-five dollars for our forty-hour week. I couldn't have spent thirty-five dollars if I'd dedicated myself to buying everything I'd ever wanted.

That check almost made the whole thing worth it. It was money for my effort. It was payment just to me, just for the results of my labor. I had worked before, helping in my family's store, and my parents gave me an allowance for spending money, but this was between me and the outside world, and I was getting my due.

That was more than fifty years ago. It sounds odd to say it that way, like many other milestones, we have no idea that we're passing them until they're in the distance far behind us. It was the worst job I ever had, and I've had a bunch of jobs. I've done factory work, washed pots, was a day laborer on a tossed salad of menial tasks, did construction, and have been a teacher for years, but I never worked harder than my summer on tobacco. Now, once a year, Social Security sends me a form letter with my benefits listed should I retire. It has a section that lists my income year by year, ever since I began to pay into it. I can't help but be especially proud of the first four hundred dollars it reports.

Scratch and Sniff

It's easy to think that everyone else is normal, and it's even easier to think that you're not. We know the workings of our own hearts. We know the thoughts that we share with no one. Chances are, if you're really like the rest of us, these things are pretty strange.

When I was in the sixth grade, I began to make up stories about numbers. I was prone to daydreams—in particular, rescue fantasies. I was forever having crushes on movie stars, characters in books, and even real live girls. These almost always involved saving some beautiful damsel from a callous and dangerous man or groups of men who were menacing her. The basic model of this scenario came from the movie *Robin Hood*, starring Errol Flynn as me, and Olivia de Havilland as the endangered but noble girl. Anyway, sixth grade marked some sort of peak for my imaginings. I think this was because I was on the verge of adolescence. I had longings that were as yet not understood, which were combined with the sheer grinding boredom of long division.

Sixth grade for me was dominated by an iron-haired teacher named Miss Shea. I'm willing to speculate that everyone has had her at one time or another. Her age was unclear. I think she'd been teaching for about ninety years. She had never married, dedicating her life to providing the world with a 180-day reprieve from eleven-year-old boys.

In her room, desks were in straight rows, and talking occurred at great peril. One of her favorite remedies for this was copying from the dictionary. Long before I'd heard of Malcolm X and his struggle to learn the English language in jail, Miss Shea had been using the copying method for the education of children. On a good day, a boy caught breaking a rule might be asked to copy a short letter—a letter that didn't have many entries. Short letters were ones like V or Y, which might be only twenty or thirty pages long. There weren't many good days. You were far more likely to be asked to copy the S or T section, the equivalent of life without parole, than to get a suspended sentence like Q or X.

Anyway, in sixth grade, I began to make up stories about numbers. I have no idea how it first began, but I remember thinking that the bravest number was Seven. Seven had a faithful retainer, Eight. Eight had been a great warrior himself, but now he was old, and he helped out Seven. Seven was in love with Four. Four was a duchess or princess or something of that nature, and she also had a retainer, Three. Three was a jolly but wise older woman, who brushed Four's beautiful long hair and advised her against going anywhere near Five.

Five was Seven's arch nemesis. Five was conniving and treacherous. He was young and strong, and had a thin, evil-looking mustache. His retainer was Six, a very evil older character, who gave very wicked advice and did unspecified awful things in the service of Five. Two was a good but mildly dimwitted foot soldier. Nine was flighty, sometimes helping Seven, sometimes Five. And One was a religious figure, possibly a saintly friar or maybe an evil Cardinal in cahoots with Five.

Throughout my struggles with the agonies of 6 into 4,326, these characters played out endless cliffhangers, with Seven vanquishing hordes of evil Five's minions, saving Four from a forced marriage or from having her school books thrown in the snow.

I never shared these stories until last summer. I was on vacation on Martha's Vineyard with my wife and daughter. As we were in the car, we somehow began to talk about how Julie and I both liked to set the temperature on our car heaters to even numbers. I added that I also liked to set them on multiples of five, and Julie said that she only liked the multiples that were even. I was suddenly reminded of my days in sixth grade, and I thought my womenfolk might be amused and impressed by my stunning feat of imagination.

As I laid out my story, the car became quieter and quieter. I thought that the girls were marveling. *How proud they must be,* I thought. Once again I had misread my own weirdness. "Dad, you're really crazy! Don't ever tell anyone about this again."

As I thought about it, it became clear that maybe it was a bit outside the box. For a short while, I wondered if I was maybe a little psychotic. Miss Shea was apt to add stress to an otherwise average day. Perhaps I'd had a breakdown, but everyone had been too busy to notice. This thought was soon dispelled and replaced by a much more comforting one: it's not that I'm outside the norm, we're *all* nuts.

As soon as I realized that, many things became much clearer. The evidence was everywhere. At my bowling league, I have a friend named Ray. Ray is a real man's man. A former tri-athlete, he has a number of investment properties that supplement the healthy pension he earns as a respected professional. He is an avid skier, is married to a lovely and bright woman, and has delightful grown children. It has been Ray's habit to bring bottles of water to his teammates. A couple of winters ago, he asked us to save the bottles for him when we were done with the contents. A perfectly reasonable request, but since he hadn't made it before, I asked him why. "For the deer," he said. Ray would have been willing to leave it at that, but now I had to know.

"What about them?" I asked.

He went on to explain that recently deer had begun to eat the plants he had around his yard. It bothered him. He set about to find ways to discourage them. His first attempt was with coyote urine. At this point, I could see that I would have to proceed with caution. "Coyote urine?"

"Yeah, I bought some and sprinkled it around the yard to repel them, but it didn't work."

Now my mind began to race. How do you know if you're getting genuine coyote urine? Could someone be selling you poodle urine instead? Where do you go to collect coyote urine? Are there farms for such things? If there are, how is it collected? Does the coyote farmer have to follow a coyote around with a bottle? Would even a domesticated, farm coyote stand for such a thing? The spinning went on and on.

I collected myself enough to go back to the original question. "So how do the water bottles fit in with this?"

Ray then took the whole thing to the next level. He explained that since coyote urine wasn't working, he was trying other urine. He was peeing in the bottles himself and leaving them around his yard. I suddenly lost my thirst. By now Ray was happy that I had shown an interest in his problem, and he went on. "I have my oldest daughter who works in a beauty salon collecting hair for me. I'm spreading it around to see how that works."

I was saved by the fact that it was my turn to bowl.

Taken at its face value, Ray's story seems really out there, but I see it another way. Ray is normal. My question just scratched the surface that he wears that covers up the oddities beneath. We all have them, but we have no occasion to show them to others. Like my number stories, they seem okay to us, and no one gives us feedback to the contrary, because no one knows they exist. Sometimes these peculiarities are so integral to our lives that we don't have any idea that they're there, let alone out of the ordinary. So forgive yourself for your foibles, and don't worry too much about those of others around you.

By the way, I owe Miss Shea a thousand thanks for all she taught me. Today I think of her sometimes in my own classroom and realize what a marvelous work ethic and sense of humor she must have had.

Young Sinatra

In the end, all we know is what we experience ourselves. We can watch others and see how they function, how they go about negotiating the world, but where does that really get us? Loved ones try to steer us toward happiness and away from folly, but nothing teaches us like our own failures. I bring this up in order to explain what I plan to say next.

Just as I was precocious in other ways, I was precocious in love. I think it was the dreamy quality I had and have that seems to attract women. At my most kind, I think it comes across as a sort of sweet vulnerability that inspires them to nurture. When I'm feeling more cynical, I think it triggers their need to see to it that men are occupied in something more practical than daydreaming or watching cable television. At least I *think* I was precocious in matters of the heart.

My first encounter with cupid came with Linda Morris, a girl who lived in my neighborhood. She wasn't the only girl around. There was Roseanne Oakes, whose parents were friends of my family and who actually lived closer than the lovely Linda. And there was Katie Panella, whose brother was one of my best friends. And there were the Gabrowski twins just across the street. Roseanne was out of the question because she once beat up Freddy Panella for calling her a girl. Katie was too young, and besides, my mother was her godmother, which made the whole thing smack of something unwholesome. The Gabrowski twins were each over two thousand pounds and were rumored to have eaten the German shepherd that mysteriously disappeared from their grandfather's farm.

Linda wasn't my choice only by default though. She had several qualities that would have made her desirable under any circumstances. There was a mystery about her that I found intriguing. For one thing, she had a sister with a different last name than hers. I had never heard of anything like that. She did her best to explain that she had a different father than her sister, but my inexperience in the world, coupled with the attention span of a fruit fly, made it all too hard to grasp. I was left with the feeling that she was somehow strange and exotic. By itself, that might have been the spark I needed to ignite my inherent masculinity, but there was something else that sealed the deal. Linda had long hair.

When I was a baby, my mother used to get me to sleep by brushing her hair against my face. The feeling was luxurious and comforting. She had thick, dark hair, kind of wavy in the style of the great movie ladies of that day. I don't know if that's why I've always been partial to long hair, but I have been, and Linda's hair was long. Truth be told, it wasn't very thick, and I can't swear that it was washed regularly, but to a mooning six-year-old, it was all it needed to be.

Our affair was short but torrid. We walked home from school together, and I showed her all the marvelous shortcuts and digressions I'd learned before I met her. I gave her the interesting pine cones and leaves I'd otherwise have given to my mother. For her part, she invited me into her home, and her mom gave me one of the cupcakes she made regularly for just such occasions. Even then I was uxorious, capable of sustaining a relationship over the long haul. We stayed together for nearly three weeks, managing the joys and strains life threw at us, "for better or worse"—until the betrayal.

I was young and didn't see it coming. I should have known that she was incapable of keeping faith. When the end came, it was like a car wreck. There I was in the cloakroom, taking off my galoshes. My coat was on its hook, my lunchbox in my cubby, and there she was. She acted as if nothing was different, as if her infidelity meant nothing, yet all the while, my world was crumbling before me. She had cut her hair! Her long, sandy hair was gone. My head reeled. No words came, but my jaw slackened. I have no idea how I made it through the day. Even recess had no power to distract me. Linda may have wondered why she walked home alone, but she said nothing about it.

Day turned to night, and day again. Life went on whether or not I was participating in it. It seemed as though the world had turned gray. Chocolate milk lost its flavor. *The Mickey Mouse Club* held no charms. It was the longest three days I'd encountered up to that point.

Time is a powerful healer, but I can't say that I ever got over Linda. I emerged an older soul, wise in the ways of rapture and pain, but some things transcend heartbreak. Fishing season started, and the world of men beckoned.

* * * * * *

Without thinking about it, I'd sworn off women. Summer vacation was filled with the eternal rhythms of fishing in the sun, walks to the library to complete my reading of the works of Dr. Seuss, and my quest to eat at least one of every candy bar in the selection at Steele's Drugstore. The world was blossoming nicely during that summer. I discovered model making and Lincoln Logs, learned to make paste out of flour and water, and built a fort under the cellar steps. But even the summer between first and second grade wasn't endless. September came and life continued.

I started second grade with a very different attitude. I wasn't a green first-grader anymore. I knew where the boys' room was and how long you could stay in there before someone came looking for you. I knew which lunch ladies gave the most gravy on the mashed potatoes. I knew which girls you could chase on the playground and which would gut you like a fish for the same thing.

I was a sophisticate. I thought of myself like a record album jacket I'd seen at Sears. It was a Sinatra album, and on the cover, he was walking down a street. There were lampposts along the way, and he had a coat carelessly slung over his shoulder. His hat was tilted on his head, and he looked like he owned the world. That's how I started second grade.

At first, that's about how things went too. My circle of friends had expanded to a size that made dodge ball a possibility. My father had opened his store, and I was assured a limitless supply of salami sandwiches, Orange Ball soda, and candy bars. My literary pursuits had blossomed to include biographies, and I had a line on Daniel Boone's life story. In the wake of the popularity of Disney's *Davy Crockett* series, this was a real coup. The future was rosy for as far as I could imagine.

I hadn't yet discovered the cyclic nature of life, and so I had no inkling of the corresponding fall to come. It started innocently enough, or at least it seemed to be innocent. We had a run of bad weather, making it impossible for us to go outside for recess. One day of indoor recess is more than enough to break the spirits of any teacher, but a four-day downpour called for extreme measures. Today, we teachers try to harness the pent-up energy of seven-year-old boys, as if they were the windmills people use now to reduce their carbon footprint. In 1957, the juvenile males were seen as being more like steam engines: they had to be vented or they'd explode.

Desperate times call for desperate measures, and that rainfall was the beginning of my second broken heart.

Our classroom was right at the corner of the back wing of the building. Our nearest neighboring classroom was the third-grade room of Miss Schultz. She and I had a history that went way back. She had only been in the school system for a year or two, and wasn't from Enfield originally. I heard that she'd grown up in Somers, a distant four or five miles away, and had gone to college in Vermont.

Everything about her was alluring. She smelled way better than Miss Mazur, my teacher, and she had what they used to call a "primary voice." This meant a sing-songy soprano that fell with dusky intimacy when she knelt by a desk to check on someone's homework. Miss Mazur, by contrast, had smoked Lucky Strikes since before Pearl Harbor and had a voice like a longshoreman. Any nurturing impulse she may have had must have evaporated decades before, when she turned eighty. Parents thought she was a good teacher because we always sat in straight rows in her room. This was considered to be the pinnacle of old-school mastery.

Miss Schultz was a newer breed. She had progressive ideas, even going so far as letting kids talk to each other between the hours of 7:30 and 2:15. Our paths had crossed in the lunchroom during the previous year, and at that time I suspected that there was a spark between us.

Anyway, indoor recess was taking a toll on everyone, but most especially on Miss Mazur. She had trained her body to go two and a half hours from cigarette to cigarette, a manageable time frame that went from morning bell to recess. As someone with seniority, she was free every recess, gratefully lumbering to the teachers' room at ten each morning, purse in hand, nicotine jones on full power. In the normal course of things, her problem began to be remedied as she opened the door, because an all-enveloping cloud of smoke billowed out every time that mysterious aperture swung open.

A digression is warranted here, to speak of the fabled teachers' room. To the students, that door shielded mysteries beyond imagination. This was a time when knowing a teachers' first name was strangely embarrassing. There was a distance between students and teachers that was unbreechable, and the teachers' room was part of it. There might have been anything going on in there, including satanic rituals or nude cliff diving. Whatever it was, smoking was a part of it.

In any event, Miss Mazur was at the end of her rope. She needed a smoke, and it was raining. In retrospect, it's clear that was the reason for the extraordinary thing that happened. Miss Mazur and Miss Schultz decided to combine classes for indoor recess and to do it in the cafeteria. The cafeteria was a multipurpose space, with tables that folded up against the walls to accommodate seating for holiday pageants, bake sales, and on the rarest occasions, indoor recess. We had never before been allowed in there to do anything but to eat lunch, but on this day, sixty second- and third-grade kids marched in two lines from our classrooms into the cafeteria.

It might be possible to keep thirty girls of that age engaged in some activity that wouldn't end in disaster, but the boys were another matter. Miss Mazur would have ruled with such intimidation that the twenty minutes of recess was in the ballpark, but how would Miss Schultz manage? We were going to find out, because once we got there, Miss Mazur slipped out to feed her addiction. The tension was palpable.

Miss Schultz was nonplussed. She calmly told everyone to line up single file and get ready for a game. She had carried a pointer from her room and was now holding it in her hand. For those who are too young to know, pointers in those days were not laser powered. They were wooden, perhaps three feet long, as thick as an adult index finger, with a conical rubber tip that looked like they could pierce steel. It seemed to be a sensible tool for her to be brandishing, given the potential for mayhem in the situation.

Much to our surprise, she climbed up onto a chair, held the pointer parallel to the floor at about six feet, and told us to run up in turn to the pointer, jump up to touch it, and continue around to the end of the line. Once everyone had a turn, she would raise the pointer two or three inches, and we'd run through it again. If someone couldn't touch the stick, they were out and had to sit against the wall until everyone had failed.

As an athlete, I was middling at best. With my academic pursuits and romantic interests, I had limited time for the finer points of kickball and the other sports played on the playground. It wasn't that I was a complete klutz; I was just a little delicate. But on that day, that special day, I rose above mediocrity. For round after round I ran and jumped, and for round after round, while others fell around me, I touched the pointer. I was sure Miss Schultz was impressed. Never had a boy jumped so high. Never had such grace been seen at Enfield Street School. It was as if I were in a dream.

As more and more failed, as the pointer rose higher and higher, I kept jumping, soaring. The rounds became shorter and shorter as the stick rose. The jumps were coming closer and closer together, and the cluster of kids waiting against the wall grew and grew. Miss Mazur had returned, looking more relieved than annoyed at the developments in the cafeteria. Her presence kept the crowd from revolting while they sat idle. They had nothing to do but watch.

Within minutes there were just three of us left: Richard Parks, a transfer student from California, where this game was probably invented, and where he had probably had private coaching from a former Olympic pointer toucher; David Swenson, that gifted athlete who lived just up the street from me; and me.

In my heart of hearts, I knew that Miss Schultz was pulling for me. I could only imagine how she must have been thrilled by my heroic leaps. (I remember seeing Mikhail Baryshnikov once in later years, and I was taken right back to that cafeteria.) Of course, such moments are necessarily fleeting. I couldn't out-jump Richard or David. I don't remember which one finally won. It didn't matter once I failed to touch the pointer.

There's no truth to the rumor that when I missed, I cried. I think it started because the cafeteria was a little dusty that day, and some of the dust got in my eyes. Anyway, when recess was over, while we were trouping back to the classrooms, Miss Schultz surreptitiously sidled up to me and said, "You did a great job of jumping today." I knew then that she was as smitten as I was. There was an age difference, sure, and she was two and a half feet taller than me, but I was willing to ignore all that for love.

Rescue fantasies began to lull me to sleep at night, dreams of evil knights, savage Indians, crazed apes, all menacing a helpless Miss Schultz, and all vanquished by me. The dreams became pretty hazy after that, fading out without further incident, but the important stuff was all fully established. Pride before a fall.

Enfield really was a small town in those days, so even though teachers were a breed apart, once in a while they could be spotted outside of their natural habitat. They might be drinking coffee at the diner before work, or they might be going to church. It was always a little disconcerting to see them, but it happened. That's what ended my dreams of the fair Miss Schultz.

Across the street from my father's store was a softball field. Men's teams, sponsored by organizations like the Rotary or Knights of Columbus, played there in season, and it was the end of the season. It wasn't exactly a big event, but on a warm night in the early fall, there wasn't much else to do. I went there because the alternative was to hang around the store. If I did that, my father would find something that needed doing, and I wasn't inspired by stocking shelves or putting away deposit bottles.

Miss Schultz and Mr. Colarusso, the bald music teacher, were at the softball field to cheer on Mr. Davis, a math teacher in the junior high, and Mr. Colarusso's roommate. They were sitting together on the bleachers—Miss Schultz in slacks and penny loafers—laughing and holding hands. It was disgraceful, right there in public, and teachers too! My heartbreak was tempered by my embarrassment and disappointment.

That was a lifetime ago. There may be a detail or two that I've forgotten or perhaps distorted. But despite the blurring of the years, the memory of betrayal remains. I've forgiven Miss Schultz her weakness, her inability to sacrifice for love. It would have been difficult for us to keep our relationship going, and she just didn't have the guts to see it through. I'm over it, and wish her well, now that she is Mrs. Colarusso, but I have to think that she feels an emptiness, a sadness, a bitterness over what she gave up.

For myself, I had only one fallback, but it was a good one. I slung my slightly dirty sweatshirt over my shoulder, tipped my baseball cap at what felt like the proper angle, and sauntered across the street to my father's store for a bottle of Orange Ball.

Spurs and Sixguns

I love westerns. I should qualify that a little and say that I love good westerns. A John Wayne or Henry Fonda movie with lots of horses and sidekicks is about the pinnacle of filmmaking as far as I'm concerned. When I was a kid, every Saturday I went to the matinee at the Strand Theatre. It was one of those ornate movie palaces that most towns had in those days. It was run by an older couple, Mr. and Mrs. Flanagan, who lived next to the library on Pearl Street. Mrs. Flanagan ran the candy counter, where you could get Black Crows, Juicy Fruits, Sky Bars, or any of the Peter and Paul candy bars for a nickel. Mr. Flanagan sold tickets and kept some semblance of order. He allowed a little scrambling before the curtain rose, and teenagers were allowed to sit close together, but "making out" was discouraged by his flashlight, as he shined it on anyone suspected of behavior that the Virgin Mary wouldn't tolerate.

The only other type of misbehavior I remember happened rarely, and that involved trying to sneak someone in through the clearly marked exit doors. When this occurred, there was a brief flash of light from the outdoors, and three or four giggling boys would hurry to blend in with the paying customers. Mr. Flanagan scored about 50 percent in capturing and ejecting these brigands, and when he did, they could be reasonably sure that their parents would be getting a call.

The Strand was no multi-screen—just one wide, Cinemascope dream stage waited behind a curtain that must have been an acre of red velvet. I'd work for the morning at my family's store, and then at noon I'd walk the quarter-mile to the movies. It was always a double feature, with cartoons and coming attractions.

The big day for most of the kids in town came on the Saturday before school started. On that day, the theater gave out fully equipped pencil boxes for all of us who would soon be returning to the world of academia. The box office line would stretch across the gravel parking lot and along in front of the police station, as we fidgeted, hollering, "No cuts!" to those bold enough to negotiate a closer place. Once inside, the scene would degenerate into a kind of joyous mayhem, as flattened popcorn boxes were frisbeed at the blank screen, and people engaged in elaborate trading schemes involving newly acquired pencil sharpeners and No. 2 Dixon Ticonderogas.

The matinee was an all-day affair. It cost thirty-five cents, up from a quarter. A large butter popcorn was fifteen cents; small was a dime. In the winter, I'd go in at twelve-thirty and come out well after dark. There was a predictable pattern to the movies shown. You'd get some combination of westerns, war movies, Tarzans, Martin and Lewis comedies, or Disneys, with a Three Stooges feature thrown in for variety.

The exception came every two months or so, when they'd show a horror double feature. As a kid, I was prone to nightmares. I don't know if I was more prone than the average kid, but we didn't talk about it to each other. We were in that idiotic stage when you had to prove your manhood by eating the hottest pepper you could find and say you liked it. Admitting to nightmares after watching scary movies was tantamount to admitting you'd always wanted to take violin lessons. It just wasn't done. For this reason, I usually kept a watchful eye on the movie marquis. I didn't want to get caught going into the movies and finding out *The Vampire That Ate the Living* and *Frankenstein's Cousin* were playing. Once in, there was no leaving. In a town as small as Thompsonville, someone was sure to notice, and sure to point it out too.

I did get stuck watching *The Man Who Turned to Stone* and *The Zombies of Mora Tau* one Saturday, and the fact that I can still remember the titles should tell you how scarred I was by the experience. My friend Marsha, with whom I was practically raised, assured me that the matinee was a Tarzan and an Audie Murphy western. She didn't want to go to the horror movies alone. I spent nearly four hours cowering in the dark, taking no comfort in the disintegration of the evildoers at the end of each film. Marsha, a much less complicated soul than I, got the appropriate giggly thrill from the experience, two or three screams and done; me, I was immobilized. Walking home in the dark was out of the question, not with monsters and aliens lurking in every shadow. We went to my parents' store, where my mother was just finishing work. She drove us. For weeks, what sleep I got was with the lights on.

Give me a good western, though, and all's well with the world. In *Shane*, when Van Heflin, pick handle raised, crashed through swinging doors to join Alan Ladd in a bar brawl, I got chills. Montgomery Clift and John Wayne's fist fight at the end of *Red River* was about as cathartic as it gets. Those were simpler times. Good was good, bad was bad, and you had no trouble knowing which was which. Never was the outcome in doubt. The only thing that ever changed was the ways in which you got to it. The good guy got the girl. The bad guy always died a fittingly violent death, and the loyal friend sidekick got drunk.

Of course, we know better today. We know that the role of the cowboy as free, honest, and forthright pioneer of wild lands is way too simple. Cowboys were just like we are today. Some must have been good, some awful, and the rest just working for a living. The "murdering red devils" who wasted the plains weren't ignorant savages impeding the progress of honest settlers. Some of those settlers were huge corporations like the railroads, which made fortunes at the expense of anyone who got in their way.

It's important that we know our true past, and that we learn from it, but there's some danger in wallowing in fully completed mistakes and injustices. I think that we sometimes get paralyzed by the feeling that we can't repay the debts we've incurred as a species and a culture. How do we make reparations for taking continents? What do we do to make up for displacing whole peoples? It's the kind of thinking that can get out of balance. We can't undo what our ancestors have done. We can't undo all that we ourselves have done out of ignorance. What we can do is make some amends for what we can, try not to do it anymore, and be just and grateful from now on. If we do those things, every now and then, we can watch Gregory Peck and Burl Ives argue about water rights and forget that your car needs an oil change or that the tuition bill is due for your daughter's school.

Where Have You Gone, Chuck Taylor?

When I was a kid, every summer day we played baseball. I'm not talking about organized, coached, scheduled baseball. Not about the kind my kids played. We played at St. Joseph's School, alongside the railroad tracks. The season started on the first seventy-degree day and continued daily until school started. The actual ritual was marked by Dave Swenson riding his blue bike up and down the street with his glove hanging on the handlebars, announcing it was time to play ball. He was more reliable than the nuclear clock. Seventy degrees, Dave Swenson, baseball at St. Joe's.

Once or twice we had one of those freak warm-ups at the beginning of March. Those were hard years, because we played until school started, no matter what. March warm-ups rarely lasted, but our season did. I suspect that a lot of us would have welcomed a couple of off days, but Dave was not only punctual, he was big and insistent. Therefore, seventy degrees, Dave Swenson, baseball at St. Joe's.

When you exclude adults from the youth recreation equation, you get something very different from what we have today. Our games rarely had more than five players on a side and usually had less than that. The teams required more arranging than a Middle East Peace Conference. We chose captains based on size. The bigger you were, the most likely you were to be captain. To choose teams, we threw a bat, and a captain caught it. The first grasp marked the point at which the other captain would place his grip. This pattern alternated until there was no bat left. The last person to have a grip got to select first from among the kids who showed up that day.

This process could be complicated if the first gripper called "topsies," which meant that the last grip would be over the top of the bat's knob. I was never big enough to be captain, so the reason why one would call "topsies" remains unknown to me. There was likely some formula involving ten-year-old calculus. If I ever see Dave Swenson at a funeral or playing bingo at the Senior Center, I'll ask him. At our age, those are the kinds of things we can still remember.

The sequence in which players were chosen was much less arcane. We knew where every kid in the town stood, with regard to baseball. The only variables possible had to do with who had shown up on a given day. The team at bat had to supply its own catcher, and if there weren't enough kids for that, we propped up a sewer grate behind home plate. Anyone around with enough equilibrium to stand up was expected to be playing. No umpires were even considered. Strikes were pitches you swung at. There were no walks.

We had some epic at bats. Jimmy V. could stand in the box for two dozen pitches, ignoring the frustrated moans from the team in the field. He insisted that the opposing pitcher was "burning it in" in a manner that was simply not sporting. Jimmy could wait. Close plays on the base paths sparked arguments that could last for days. It was a very rare day indeed when both teams could agree on the score. Foul balls were easy: Over the right-field fence was foul. Into the asphalt in left field was foul. We had a fence for home runs, but the only kid to ever hit one was from California visiting relatives, and we didn't let him play anymore after that.

Before you get the impression that baseball was fun for us, let me clear a few things. First and foremost, I was a year younger than most of the other kids. When they were eleven, I was ten. When they were twelve, I was eleven. You get the picture. One year now, at age fifty-nine, means almost nothing. At ten, it's a chasm. I lacked almost every physical skill needed to play well. When I learned to finally throw all the way to the plate, the other kids needed to move it to accommodate their newfound strength. I always swung so late at pitches that I was forever hitting foul balls over the right field fence. This was a complicated problem, because the other side of the fence was high grass, railroad tracks, and a fifty-foot drop into the Connecticut River. Balls hit over that fence were almost always lost balls. I was required to supply my own ball, just in case it was lost. I was picked nearly last every time. To this day, I remember with gratitude, Mikey Flynn and Angelo DeBona, the only two younger (and worse) than me.

You might wonder why I exposed myself to sure humiliation and frustration. It might have been because I had a sense of pride; I was going to show Dave and the others that I could be as good as they were. It could have been for the love of the game during the summer that Roger Maris and Mickey Mantle were rewriting the record books. Maybe I had an overwhelming longing to be accepted by my peers and wanted to demonstrate my willingness to sacrifice for a friend.

All of these reasons had nothing to do with the real driving forces. The fact was, I had no choice. Here's where you have to listen carefully. It wasn't having no choice because I was forced to do it. I had no choice because that was all we ever imagined we could be doing. We had three television stations, two of which had the same shows.

Our parents had all grown up with each other, had worked and played together during the Depression, and the expectation was that we would "play out" as long as no volcanoes erupted within three houses of ours. They knew who we were with, where we were, and that we would be home in time to eat dinner. We didn't have tennis lessons. We didn't practice piano. We didn't go to tutoring. If you weren't getting good grades, it just meant you were going to work in the local carpet factory until you were seventy or so, a reasonable life in those days.

We played baseball without examining the efficacy of it. We played baseball without weighing the alternatives we were missing by doing so. Today it seems that every choice kids make means a dozen opportunities missed.

I remember the first time I was faced with a choice. It seemed like the first time I had control over anything in my life. That was the year that Chuck Taylors became important. If you weren't barefoot, you were wearing sneakers (except on Sunday at church). The choice was complex because Chuck Taylors came in black or white, and high or low top. The permutations were staggering. I wanted to be sure that I didn't screw this up. I only got sneakers once a year, unless I had an unnatural growth spurt. Having to live with the wrong sneakers for a year was unthinkable. The solution: whatever Dave Swenson picked.

I often wonder if we fill our lives with unnecessary choices. We place so much import on our options that we invariably feel disappointed and cheated by the "roads not taken," rather than enjoying our decisions. We should face the fact that there really is little difference between high and low, black and white.

It's nearly seventy degrees. Let's play ball.

Diners' Club

My father was generous…to a fault. He could be the most charming host anyone ever saw. He reveled in showing off the house he built with his own hands and unfailingly insisted that anyone who visited share dinner. For much of my life, there was never a day at my house when less than a dozen people stopped in, were fed, and were entertained with stories, healthy arguments, and small gifts. I should probably mention that my mother was the one who did the cooking and made the endless coffee that was served and cleaned up after these impromptu parties. I know she didn't mind much. It was always better to have my father occupied than for him to have nothing to do.

With nothing to do, Dad always did something, and that could spell disaster. His head was filled with improvements and experiments for our lives. He usually worked on them on Sunday, because that was the day his store was closed. He always had something going, and it was rarely a little job. We built an extra bath and bedroom on the west side of the house. We built a kitchen with two hearths and a beehive brick oven. We rehabbed the house next door that he bought from our cranky neighbor. These tasks always took at least six months, and I was always expected to "help."

These were days of living hell for me. He was not one to hold in feelings of frustration, so his projects were punctuated by curses, muttering, and banging that sent Mom and me cringing. I especially hated these days. He would send me looking for a three-sixteenths-inch, deep-socket wrench or a cross peen Warrington hammer, and I would know that if I had fifty years I couldn't find it in the warren that was his tool room. I'd obediently shuffle down to our basement, open drawers, boxes, and cabinets, shift the pile of saws or wing nuts or whatever else was close by, and then return empty-handed, prepared to take my beating.

He'd stalk down the stairs himself, with me sheepishly behind him. "Jesus Christ, what the hell is wrong with you! It's right here next to the Stillson wrench by the bolt cutter, where I told you." We'd then go back to the job, with me standing silently while he "showed me how to install a hardwood floor" or how to cut the rafters for a hip roof. I literally watched for hours while he worked mostly silently or cursed or asked me to run the fool's errand of finding something for him.

I now understand him better. I curse while I work too. It relieves the tension I build up while trying to do manual labor. It's not directed at anyone, and it doesn't even mean that I'm angry. On the contrary, it sometimes comes when I'm really enjoying solving some problem and a new element pops up. Marcie and Julie get on me for it. I understand how uncomfortable it must make them, because it made me miserable.

I try to tell them that it has nothing to do with them, but I know they shouldn't have to tolerate it, so I try to stop. Ironically, my father was just about as happy as he could get at the end of one of these days. He'd rub his hands together and clap them. He'd take us out for hot dogs, bowling, or just for a ride somewhere. Just like me, he'd go back frequently to see the work he'd accomplished, and I know his mind would start to work on the next stage of the job. I know he couldn't wait for Sunday, just like I can't wait sometimes to finish a birdhouse or a toy box. We're a lot alike in some ways.

I also love to host, but maybe not as often as my dad. I love having Walter and his family, our friends Matt and Sue, or Kerry, Jason, and their kids over to watch a special football game or to use our pool. I revel in cooking for them all, as well as plenty of other people we've "accumulated" over the years. I picture myself as a kind of uncle who offers serious advice, talks silly to the kids, and tells "back in the day" stories to the other oldsters around.

The fact is, I love my own home. I love my own cooking. I love my own special chair, my own brand of Italian bread, and my own bathroom. It's the place where I'm most comfortable—and most in charge—and that something is a key to my father and me. It's not just generosity that prompts me to host. It's at least partly selfishness. I don't like to let anyone feel that I'm beholden to them, that they have some hold on me. It feels a little like dependency, and that makes me nervous.

I know right where that comes from. My father made it an ironclad point never to take anything from anyone, and that extended to the rest of his family. If his partner at the store gave me a dollar for four hours of work on Saturday, I knew that I was to politely but adamantly refuse it. Tips for carrying grocery bags were absolutely taboo. He had to be in control, and that meant he could give but not receive.

Recently I called Kerry and Jason to invite them over to our home. The weather had been good, and the pool was open. They have two spectacular kids, and we get to feel like practice grandparents. Several years previously, Kerry had invited my family to their home, and I had impulsively told her that I was old and cranky and didn't like traveling to other peoples' homes, but that I loved to see them. From that point on, we saw each other at my house. I felt myself "holding court" in the familiar comfort of my own couch, and I liked it.

When Kerry answered the phone this time, she invited my family to her house, and I had a revelation. A truly generous spirit allows others to do for them. It's a gesture of trust and friendship. I'd been asking these people (and lots of others) to allow me to maintain my own sense of worth and control at their expense. I wasn't being mean, just emotionally lazy and selfish.

We went to their house and had a lovely night. I think they enjoyed showing us their home, sharing the food they made, and having us sit in their chairs. Jason gave me a baseball cap with the logo of their town yacht club. This was a particularly important gesture, given that they have no body of water in their town. I know why he did it, though, and I think it makes our families' friendship deeper.

Yin and Yikes

For centuries, people have said that it's impossible to understand the opposite sex. I can't say for sure that women can understand men; after all, I'm not a woman. I can say that it's not that hard for a man to understand women. I can do it, and now I'm going to tell you how.

First, men and women don't just learn to be different; we're born that way. Little boys find a way to make toy guns (or spears or clubs or whatever phallic extenders their particular social experiences provide for them) without being told to. Parents who try to raise peaceful, gentle boys may as well chain them in the basement from birth. You can't change the nature you're born with. Girls will have tea parties of some sort no matter where they're from. (My friend Larry has great, interesting, successful kids, and I asked him if there was anything a parent can do to shape their children. He said of course they can, but not on purpose.) These are atavistic, ingrained patterns that have evolved to provide us all with our optimum chance of overcoming whatever cave bears come our way, storing the wild seeds we've gathered, and surviving. The lesson here is that as long as we're going to be who we are anyway, we may as well make the best of it.

Most of the differences we're born with don't bring us into many conflicts until puberty. Up until then, we don't have many instances in which we mix with women who aren't our mothers or their surrogates (elementary school teachers, crossing guards, etc.). Once we hit puberty, however, the plot thickens. First, nature sends us what should be a clear message. Twelve-year-old females suddenly get four inches taller than twelve-year-old males. What the boys should be getting from this is that we're about to be pushed around; there's not much we can do about it, so we may as well get used to it.

It's important to note here that the pushing around that's going to occur is necessary pushing around. Women aren't bossy by some caprice. Without them paying attention to what has to be done, we men would be off in the garage inventing the wheel so that we could cruise some prehistoric drive-through, while the communal fire bundle burns itself out. The lesson here, guys, is that, for the most part, women know what's best for all of us. A good relationship with a woman is one in which she allows a man to preserve the external illusion that he is making the important decisions.

The device that nature has developed for us to be able to maintain this illusion is called romance. *Romance*, remember, is a word that refers to Romans, the group that conquered much of Europe, North Africa, and parts of Asia a couple of thousand years ago. They ate weird things, enjoyed entertainments like throwing criminals to wild beasts, and put pornographic murals on their walls. Roman citizens were men. Women were not allowed citizenship.

I've concluded, therefore, that men are more romantic than women. This conclusion is based on more than this historical connection. Men truly are more romantic than women in the poetry-flowers-walking on the beach sense too. This goes back to the puberty thing also. Women learn early on that they are going to be having babies. Not much romance to that, let me tell you. If there is a messier process, I can't think of it. And childbirth classes are not for the faint of heart. The wives watch and listen to information about meconium, cervical dilation, and expelling the placenta, while the fathers-to-be sit in horror at the thought of what they might have to see. They tell you to bring a pillow so that the pregnant women can be comfortable, but all the ladies know that it's to muffle the screams of the traumatized men.

Before we go too far, romance is a good thing. Women like it, sometimes. Knowing what and when can make or break a relationship. In early relationships, it's okay to start with some kind of show of interest. Pubescent boys know this instinctively. What this show of interest should be, they don't know. Many think that throwing food at girls in school cafeterias or walking in awkward groups behind groups of seven-foot-tall, frosted-blond eighth-graders will serve to alert females that a breeding-eligible mate is in the area. The successful few (and there are very few) have a gene that tells them that the proper mode of expression in this stage is disinterest. Not grubby-handed, look-at-the-size-of-this-night crawler disinterest, but I-like-women-and-am-definitely-breeding-eligible-but I'm-not-that-interested-in-you disinterest.

A mentor of mine named Ed once told me that one should "never pursue a distancer." This meant that if someone liked running away, you probably couldn't catch her by chasing her. As I lived with this idea for a few years, I found that the converse was also true. If you walked away from a distancer, it piqued her interest, and she tended to chase you.

Now, in life, there are some rare individual men who just seem to know this. Nature wants them to breed because when the rest of us were dreading the showers in gym class, they were shaving twice a day. For them, eighth grade is like hunting on one of those ranches in Texas where they hand-raise animals for others to shoot. They are the subject of over 90 percent of all text messages sent by females, right until eleventh grade.

Between eighth and eleventh grade, the rest of us have to live and learn. There is no way to teach a man when to be romantic and when to shut up and look serious. That's the bad news. The good news is that women and greeting card companies will tell you, if you listen carefully. If you do, any woman will wisely allow her man to take credit for knowing when the bedroom needs to be repainted lavender or for buying tickets for the Van Gogh exhibit for your anniversary.

The eighth- to eleventh-grade gap is something to consider, if you want to really understand women. In that time, individual boys begin to grow, mature, and brush their teeth regularly without being told. As they do, the girls who have chosen them carefully cull them from the herd along the fence at the football game. These boys have been selected to start their training as husbands and fathers. They fawn and stutter in the presence of the girl who has picked them, until she decides her part is done, and then they break up. This period can last anywhere from a week to a couple of years, depending on the amount of effort required in his education and the genuine connection that really can exist in this "first love" period. Like Marine basic training at Parris Island, it's an essential period of agony and magic. Semper Fi.

The information gathered during first love remains forever. Most men never recover fully, and some never recover at all. We learn the hurt look of our uneducated buddies' faces when we decline to go out egging houses on Halloween with them, because we're going to dye Easter eggs with our honey's family. We develop calluses on our ears talking on the phone about nothing we can even identify five minutes after we hang up. We learn about intimacy and loyalty and depths of jealousy we had no inkling we could harbor. We learn about cleaving to another who isn't a family member or teammate, and ultimately we learn about letting go. All vital lessons if one is to go on and become a whole adult.

The rest is pretty much waiting until you get found by the next woman and hopefully on until marriage, old age, and death. Getting found, however, warrants a little time. In the 1960s, my friend Jay and I (along with my friend Gary and assorted others) went on the hunt for the women who would find us. This seemed at the time to be something of a done deal. Jay had a car—a 1966 Ford Galaxy 500, with a V-8 engine, dual exhausts, and the first eight-track stereo player anyone had ever seen. We had no visible deformities and had learned all about the facts of life from a guy who lived near us who had visited his cousin in New York. Any more would be overtraining.

We got on our bellbottoms and prepared to love. Night after night we drove around our town. We went from the McDonald's to the Friendly's. We drove by the houses in which we knew girls lived. We drove to the deserted high school parking lot and laid rubber. We went everywhere possible to disperse our pheromone-laden scents, but nothing! Days, weeks, a whole summer—and nothing. Where were the women?

Jay, who had less staying power than the rest of us, was the first to drop by the wayside. One Friday night, he called and said that he was staying home. He whimpered something about his mother making meatloaf and bowed out. With no alternative (my father's Buick could never get girls the way Jay's Ford could), I accepted his offer and joined them.

There are moments when God decides to enlighten the ignorant. That night, Jay's father, a lawyer, had a client in his home office. This client brought her daughter, a cute, smart sixteen-year-old with whom Jay and I had a passing acquaintance in school. She had nothing to do while her mother prepared her will or sued a neighbor or whatever she was doing. Jay was a polite host, and suddenly, in his family room, watching *Hogan's Heroes*, Jay was selected. A brilliant example of never pursue a distancer.

My own selection was more conventional. Junior prom was approaching. I had begun taking showers regularly. A friendly female sophomore who sat behind me in biology became noticeably friendlier. I told Gary. Gary told a sophomore girl in his chemistry class. She relayed the message to the biology sophomore that I had noticed her increased friendliness—and the recent removal of her braces, which was an inadvertent master stroke. The chemistry sophomore told Gary that the biology girl would welcome an invitation to the prom. I told Gary that I would tell the biology sophomore.

The chemistry sophomore arranged a meeting at her home for a Friday-night party, complete with her overprotective, old-country Italian parents and at least sixty Letterman albums. Transportation and security was arranged through another series of intermediaries. The meeting came off without a hitch, prom date secured, and the rest is history. Gary and the chemistry sophomore have three grown children, and they recently celebrated their thirtieth anniversary.

What, finally is to be learned from all this?

1. We are who we are. We're born that way, and we can't substantially change it. Get used to it. Accept yourself.

2. Women are more like men than men know. If we don't annoy them too much and put ourselves in places where we feel comfortable and where they might be around, a good one will find us and take us home.

3. Bathing helps.

GPS

    I like to make plans. I like to think about the things ahead and be prepared for them. I like to make lists and cross off things as I do them. It's all part of feeling like I'm in control of my life. It's okay that I do these things, because I know that I'm just kidding myself. I remember reading that if you want to make God smile, make plans. I think it's a good idea to make God smile. You never know when that can pay off.
    For the last thirty-five years, I've been a teacher. Well, mostly a teacher. It would be more accurate to say that I've worked in schools. In the education biz, what I've done is usually referred to as "direct service." I've taught all the traditional subjects, along with electives like home ec, French, health, the history of World War I, and what seems like a thousand other things. I've been a "child care worker", which translates into tantrum control. I've supervised enough field trips to the Museum of Science to qualify as a founding member. The economy isn't great for career changes right now, so I think I'm going to stick with "mostly teaching" for a while more.
    I didn't plan to be a teacher. I actually didn't plan to be anything. I slogged through college in the sixties and seventies, taking a mere seven years to complete a four-year degree. It was a winding road with detours to make vending machines, clean ducts in factories, work in a nursery (the plant kind), and live off the Boston landscape as was pleasantly possible during the Age of Aquarius. I pretended to be a rebel, all the while obediently calling home every Sunday, and I waited for life to let me know what was in store for me.

Actually, life for me at that time was sort of a blur, with moments of intense guilt swirling with periods of insane pleasure. I never could quite shed the conscience (or fear) that came from being raised on Annette Funicello while living in a Grace Slick world. I grew my hair, read very serious books, slept often in the back of the 1967 Chevy station wagon my parents bought me, and tried to enlist in the battle that was the sexual revolution. It was an exciting time to be alive, with civil rights struggles, cities burning, national student strikes closing universities, draft resisters, anti-war protesters, and artistic pioneers like the Beatles echoing and leading the charge.

My own political stand peaked during the spring of 1971. I had one badge that read "Vietnam for the Vietnamese" and another with a white dove on a blue background that read "Peace." I marched on the Boston Common with tens of thousands of others. (It was a beautiful spring day, and I had a new Frisbee.) I voted for Eugene McCarthy, even though he was clearly going to be a loser, and I got drafted.

There was no way that I was fit to be a soldier. I was afraid of the dark, couldn't run ten feet without wheezing, cringed at using a communal shower, got nosebleeds, and hated no one enough to want to yell at them, let alone shoot them. There had to be some sort of mistake.

Actually, what happened was this. There was a draft lottery. One night, all of America turned on the television and watched as balls were pulled from a drum. The balls had the three hundred and sixty-six possible days of the year printed on them. The position in which your birthday was selected determined the order in which you would be called up for military service. I was in the very first lottery, and my number was 143. It was estimated that the first two thirds of the birthdays would be taken. One forty-three was sure to be called.

This wasn't as dire as it sounds. I was a student, remember. I could get my induction deferred, as long as I remained in good standing. I had two years to put things off, and a lot can happen in two years.

A lot did happen, and in a lot less than two years. It wasn't easy to remain a student in good standing when you were failing four of five classes. In fact, it not only wasn't easy, it wasn't possible. My student advisor told me that the best I could do was to withdraw from the university. That would allow me to return in a year if I'd taken courses somewhere to make up for lost credits. This was a drill I knew. I was a regular in summer school; it was what had kept me around as long as I had.

In January, just before the exams I would have failed, I withdrew. Now, in September when the school year started, we filled out draft forms, requesting our deferments. They usually came promptly in March. I was anticipating the same time frame would apply to my newly changed status. My advisor hinted that my changed status wouldn't be reported to my draft board until the end of the school year. Six months from application to action. Since I was planning to return at the beginning of the next fall, the six-month turnover rate should just about hold me. I'd be back in good standing before the devil knew I was dead. I was making plans.

I left the first week in January, and by the third week, I had my new One A draft status, and a week after that, I was called up for my physical. Welcome to the funhouse. My father drove me to the train station in Hartford. The state of Connecticut generously provided a railroad car to take all the inductees to the draft board in New Haven. It was five in the morning, and the car was filled with bewildered, frightened, muttering youths, all riding together into the sunrise.

There were people with plans among us. One guy ate a whole pound of butter while the train pounded along the tracks. He claimed it would read as high cholesterol, and get him out. Two or three others wore makeup. Not too much, just a little eye shadow, some subtle blush, and a bit of lip gloss. Don't ask, don't tell wasn't a policy they supported. Most of us were just so weirded out by the whole scene that we were paralyzed.

When we arrived in New Haven, they had us strip to our underwear, put our important belongings in an olive-drab drawstring bag that we could carry, and divided us into two equal groups. One group underwent some sort of intelligence testing that I assume was meant to determine whether or not you might be officer material. The instructions to this test were given by a sergeant from Mississippi or Arkansas or some other Southern state. He was aware that his accent might be confusing for us New Englanders, so he immediately stated that he would "say everything twice say everything twice," and he did just that. It was obvious that he had given these instructions often, because the words flowed from him flowed from him without him having to look at any written notes any written notes.

In a big room filled with rectangular folding tables, along with perhaps a hundred other young men who had awakened at four in the morning, with drawstring bags hanging from our wrists, in our underwear, we took intelligence tests intelligence tests.

After our group finished the intelligence portion of our evaluation, we saw the medical staff for tests. I'm pretty sure that many of the people who prodded us weren't full doctors; most seemed to be medics or something. None seemed particularly interested in what they were doing. We stood in an endless winding row, stepped into the next available cubby to have our eyes examined, our medical records scanned, our hearing checked. And we were tested to see if we could cough with our heads turned to the side. Some of the others had letters from doctors claiming various ailments that should disqualify them from service. They seemed like Peter Lorre, pleading to the disinterested tester, "Oh please sir, there has been a terrible mistake."

By now, I felt like I was in one of those strange amoeba light shows that were popular at rock concerts at the time. The scene before me was unlike anything I'd seen before or since. Eventually, my turn at the cubby came up. I sat in my tighty whities while a bored twenty-five-year-old strapped me into a blood pressure cuff. He squeezed once and read. He squeezed again, read again, and said, "Why didn't you say that you have high blood pressure? Why are you wasting our time?"

Wasting *their* time?! He sent me to an isolated bench, told me to get dressed, and left me there. I couldn't even hope that this meant I was out. I knew I wasn't deserving of the blessing of high blood pressure, but there it was.

I don't even remember the trip home. All I know is that six months later I got my reclassification, One Y. If the Vietnamese decided to invade Connecticut, I might be called upon to fight; otherwise, I was out.

I sincerely hope that this doesn't come off as deprecatory to those who served in Vietnam. At the time, many hurtful and ignorant things were said about the hundreds of thousands of brothers and sisters who went there and did what they believed was called for. It was more than a serious situation; I was just incapable of seeing it that way at the time. Like I said, I had no plan. That's just where the tide swept me.

Most of us want a clear set of directions. That's why we all love our GPS. We want to have some idea of the future and the feeling that we have something to say about it. Just enough of the time, we are allowed to keep the illusion, but as soon as we put all our important belongings in the drawstring bag in preparation to move on, something jumps up.

The other side of the picture is more like plunge and pray. This calls for a kind of faith and surrender. Every once in a while you have to just leap and see where you land. In fact, that's how I started teaching. I had a friend named Dick. He started a year behind me at Boston College and finished a year or so ahead of me. He had a job at a school for seriously disabled teens and young adults, and he talked about it constantly.

I was living in a dorm room that belonged to a guy we called Dirty Phil. I was waiting for final grades to be posted and for my degree to be finished finally. Phil emerged from a drunken stupor one afternoon and asked Dick if he could arrange for him to be interviewed for a job. Dick moved heaven and earth to set up a meeting with his school's assistant director the following day. It seems there were two weeks left in their school year, and they needed a little help cleaning up around the edges.

The next day came—apparently a surprise for Phil. He wasn't ready. In fact, he wasn't there. Dick was up a creek. His assistant director was expecting an interview, was coming in early for just that reason. Dick was a good friend. I offered to go instead of Phil. It couldn't be worse than cleaning ducts.

That was thirty-five years ago. I'm still plunging. I'll let you know when I hit bottom.

For the Want of a Nail

I was named after my grandfather. That's the Sicilian way. The first son is named for the father's father, first girl for his mother. The maternal grandparents don't come in until later—second son, mother's father; second daughter, mother's mother. In large families, you can end up with four cousin Sals. It's almost like keeping a family Bible. You can trace generations like that.

I was the only grandson to be named Vincent. It wasn't because there weren't opportunities. My father had three brothers, and they each had a son. My five aunts had sons, too, but they had obligations to their husbands' families, so their lapses in the naming department are kind of excusable.

In retrospect, it explains a lot to me. Although I was very young when he died, I always felt like I was my grandfather's favorite. He'd tear up when I came into his faded living room, and say "Veni ca, Vincenzo!" He'd hand me a fifty-cent piece and smile, smile, smile. My cousins were pretty welcome, too, but no tears, and usually just a nickel. For a long time I wondered why my cousins didn't like me. Now I know.

The act of my naming echoed further than just my relationship with my cousins. My father was showing respect in a way that pleased his father—and rankled some of his siblings. That wasn't entirely out of character for Dad. Rankling was one of his many talents. In fact, some say that he brought it to heights previously unknown. He had that kind of personality. He contrasted Old World grace with New York brass.

He had fought with some of his brothers and sisters, and in their eyes, it was one and done. There were no second chances. If you did something they thought was out of line, that was it. My father and one of his brothers were next-door neighbors for forty years, and they didn't speak for the last thirty-five of them. They would mow the lawn wheel to wheel and not acknowledge the other's presence. They don't just hate 'em like they used to.

Anyway, my name is Vincent. As a kid, you don't get too much say in how that's used. At first, some of my father's friends began to call me Jimmy. It seems that second-generation Italians wanted American names, so they tolerated the old-school formalities but bent them to fit the new world. I had a friend named Sammy for years as a kid, but when we got to junior high school and the teacher took attendance, he shocked me by answering "Here" to the name Salvatore.

"Jimmy" turned out to be just a close call, though. My quiet, behind-the-scenes Irish mother let it be known that if she wanted a Jimmy, she would have named me James. Back to Vincent.

Well, Vincent is too much name for a kid. The dentist's assistant might call you that when it's your turn, but no one else does. It's kind of a "good shoes" name, the kind you dust off for occasions, but you don't play in them. For a long time, I was Vinny. On my little street, there were three Vinnys in just a few houses. One was a grown-up, and was even Irish, so he didn't count. The other was my friend Vinny Perino. He was a year older than me, but we were close. My parents were his sister's godparents, and that meant that we were god brothers, or at least god stepbrothers. The point is, I didn't think too much about my name during those years.

Vinny is a pretty safe name too. People view Vinnys as nice boys who do what their mothers tell them to do. Vinnys go to church, go to confession and communion, and do their best not to have impure thoughts. Lots of Vinnys become priests. In any case, Vinny stayed through high school.

High school was a time fraught with anxiety and peril. Would I do okay in my classes? Would I get a girlfriend? Would bigger, older boys humiliate me in the hall? Would I get my driver's license? Would I get a girlfriend? Would I get into a good college? Would I get a girlfriend?

On and on it went. I can't say that I'd volunteer to do it over again, but I made it through and on to college.

Here is where I could have taken another path. This would have been the moment that could have changed everything. I just didn't see it at the time, and I missed the opportunity that might have made all the difference. I could have been Vince. Vince. Vince is a very different name from Vinny. Vinces are worldly and maybe a little dangerous. Vinces are thin and are cool without trying. People pursue Vinces, hoping to be seen with them. Girls are a little afraid of Vinces, but they are drawn to them like pit bulls to pork chops. No, I take that back. Girls aren't afraid of Vinces. They're afraid of themselves when Vinces are around, because they lose all inhibitions.

In the moment when I left home and came to school in Boston, no one knew I was a Vinny. It was my moment to choose my future. I didn't even see it coming, and then it was gone.

Life can sometimes turn on a second. I started college as a roomer in a private home off campus. I had three housemates when I arrived, and we introduced ourselves. In that critical moment, I extended my hand and said, "Glad to meet you, Jim. I'm Vin." Vin, a compromise of a name. It's not a bad name, really. Vin can be grown up. Vin can wear a suit jacket to dinner and look okay. You can borrow a snow shovel from a Vin and be confident that if you return it late, he'll understand. But girls don't get that uncomfortable, delicious animal feeling from a Vin. Men don't race each other to invite Vins over to watch pay-per-view fights. Like I said, a compromise of a name.

For a while, I had to work to come to grips with the enormity of my missed opportunity. I regretted not being able to live the James Bond fantasies I dreamed while becoming who I finally am. The good news is that finally, I am a Vin. I'm comfortable without the mystery an adolescent wishes for. A Vin can live gracefully without adventure. At my age, a Vince is a little tired; it's a burden to have to be cool at sixty. The dentist's assistant calls you Vincent again, even though you ask her to call you Vince. She thinks you're just a polite, aging man, and out of respect uses the name your grandfather used.

FRIENDSHIP, MARRIAGE, and CHILD-REARING

Baby Steps

My friend Steve has cancer. Pancreatic cancer. That's one of the bad ones. I know because my friend Diane died of it just a few months ago and because once you get to be my age, you become acquainted with lots of things that are bad to have.

When I heard about Steve, I got very philosophical. I started to think that everyone gets something that will kill them. For sure, Steve was a surprise, because he has always been so healthy. He was a Marine, earned a black belt in taekwondo, played soccer most weekends, and had more energy than most kids. He and his family came often to our house, especially in summer, when we had our pool open. Steve would spend hours outplaying the six-year-olds, inventing silly games like jumping up to prove the earth was spinning, and they naturally loved him for it.

I've come to rationalize that dying is in all of our futures, but for some of us the timing seems wrong. I would have thought that Steve would be one of those settled old men who drive too slowly and wear bucket hats, but that isn't likely to be the case.

I've heard that the Dalai Lama says that when good people die young, their purpose on earth is to teach those of us who remain behind. I've been willing to believe that, and even more so now. Diane taught me that people who are dying are still people who are living, and Steve has taught me that people who are living are also people who are dying.

My first impulse when I hear that something like this has happened is to wonder what I can do about it. Cancer is so final. It's the punctuation mark that trumps all other subjects and predicates. In the face of it, I become immobilized. I can't cure it. I can't make it better. I want to take out a magic wand and take it away, so that everything is fine. But I can't. I imagine that all will be tears and anger. I imagine that Steve will be full of bitterness at the cosmic unfairness of it all, at the dispassionate condemnation that cancer brings, despite the good acts of a lifetime. I picture Steve withered and doddering, obsessed with medical jargon and pathetic striving. What can I do in the face of all that?

Life is full of surprises. Some scientist finds some living organism on the rim of a volcano or a couple of sunburned sailors are found on a raft two months after a shipwreck, and for just a moment we let ourselves believe in miracles. Sadly, our belief is soon buried in the rhythm of everyday life. We lose sight of the divine as we wait in grocery store lines or watch baseball games, and we find ways to lose sight of the passage of our few moments on earth.

And then there's Steve. At first, it seemed that he and his family wanted to keep things quiet. They needed to have their privacy to work out treatment options and to come to grips with the new facts of their lives. An occasional phone call kept my conscience clear and denial intact.

Distance works just fine for me, but not for my wife, Marcie. She's my opposite in many ways. When problems strike, I slow down and think, and she speeds up and acts. My way is better sometimes, her's others.

Marcie did more than call, she visited, and she had some real skills to offer. Marcie is a financial planner, and she could comfort Steve by helping arrange his finances so that he could feel that his family wouldn't suffer after he was gone. I teach English and history. I could correct his grammar.

Despite my impotence, Steve asked for me. I didn't really expect it, but neither was it a surprise, so I dutifully visited with Marcie. And I was once again granted a glimpse of something bigger than ourselves. Steve was Steve. Thinner, grayer, but Steve. He didn't want to talk about T-cell counts or radiation treatments; he wanted to talk about car repairs and game shows. It was easy to joke and laugh with him, just as it had always been.

Next came his stroke.

Pancreatic cancer spreads, and his had done just that. In the hospital, his wife, Kathy, saw his eyes roll and heard his slurred speech. Kathy is a nurse, so she knew it was a stroke. It wasn't something exactly unexpected. I imagine it's like one of those funhouse rides where you know startling things are going to jump out at you, but you just don't know when.

Now Steve is paralyzed on his left side. Soccer player, martial artist, Marine rugby player, now bed rider. The funny thing is, he now seems more alive than before. More Steve than before. He has ideas about how to help people in worse shape than him. He remembers jokes about scuba divers in forest fires, and he teaches us just as the Dalai Lama said.

He's given me a gift that Diane gave too. He talks about the power of little things, the power of neighborly visits to defeat cancer. Cancer, whose mission is to defeat life, is defeated itself by the simple act of living. Living people eat soup together and talk about football and remember when their kids were small together. My friend Steve doesn't let me forget that he's living, and that I'm living and that we have gifts to give each other that can't cure cancer, but that can defeat it.

Steve has an idea. He wants to run a marathon. He doesn't have one of those fancy racing wheelchairs. As a matter of fact, he couldn't maneuver one if he did. His idea is kind of like baby steps, a team of ordinary people, each taking fifty steps, pushing him along the twenty-six-mile route. Ordinary people can take fifty steps, and ordinary people can defeat the loneliness of cancer. They can defeat the dehumanizing hunger of cancer. Ordinary people can defeat the indignity of cancer.

I know. Steve and Diane have shown me.

Mr. Lucky

I've been blessed with pretty good self-esteem. I don't see much of a reason for it. I'm basically an overweight, lazy guy pushing sixty. I don't look like Brad Pitt. I can't play piano or run a mile. The few things I'm good at aren't that fabulous. My wife says that I make good lasagna. I'm an excellent bowler…. Well, there are other things I should be able to mention here, but they don't immediately come to mind, so I'll move on.

There is one area in which I think I'm exceptional. It's not something that I can take a lot of credit for. It's not something I've earned or sacrificed for in any way. I'm a very lucky man.

I'm not exceptionally lucky in the traditional ways. I did once find a wallet with forty dollars in it, but I had to split the money four ways with the people I was with at the time. I got a scratch lottery ticket worth a thousand dollars, but I must have spent three thousand on losers first. My luck has come in other ways. I have a great family. My wife is terrific; my kids have survived the mean suburban streets of middle-class America and have become smart, productive, empathetic adults. My mother and sister are healthy and as happy as any of us have a right to expect. My job has been interesting and satisfying—let me tell you, that's a blessing—and I have friends.

Today it seems like people need to be surrounded by as many others as possible. They seem to like the density of crowds. Lately, this tendency is magnified by an avalanche of technology that lets us have thousands of "friends." We even have a new verb, *friend*, as in, to friend someone. I must admit that I've remained in the dark about MySpace,

Facebook, and now Twitter. My interest in technology peaked when we got cable television. I've mastered my remote control, and now I'm basking in the possibilities of DVRing.

I should admit that I have succumbed to a few pressures regarding the world of the future. I've sent three emails, and read at least that many that have been sent to me. I bought a used car that has a camera that lets you see where you're going when you back up, and I find I like doing that. I'm also willing to concede that if I keep on breathing, I'll probably pick up on some more of these "innovations," but I guarantee that I won't do it willingly.

For the last several years I've noticed that whenever I learn something new, I forget something old. It's like when your cupboard is full, and you have to put one more thing in it. Something else has to go. I have no say over what I forget, and that can be troublesome. Two years ago I had to call my friend Carol twice in a week to get my own phone number. Anyway, suffice it to say that I haven't "friended" anyone in the nontraditional sense.

As I was saying, I have friends. In life, a normal person needs to have at least one real friend. You can get through childhood with one other kid who knows everything there is to know about dinosaurs or who loves horses. That one friend is a refuge from the world's messages that you're strange if you build model railroads or talk on ham radios. It's easy to feel strange if you're paying attention to the things we're told we're supposed to be doing. With a friend, we get to see that someone else—someone who could pass for normal in our estimation—likes what we like or hates what we hate. It means that we might be normal too.

There's no telling where friendship may be planted, but it's nurtured in daily living and harvested in crises. You build it at cookouts and while watching football games on television. Its roots are grounded with borrowed wheelbarrows and jokes about bulging waistlines, and its shade protects us through storms and sunlight.

Yes, I'm an extraordinarily lucky man. I have two friends. I'm a little troubled about saying that, because I also have people in my life who I know would "be there for me" if I ever needed them—fine, generous people who I love and admire. Some I have known for many years; they were at my wedding and would care for my family if I wasn't able to. I don't want to hurt any feelings by suggesting that they aren't friends in the way that I'm speaking about. I think it's because I haven't been enough of a friend to them, haven't allowed them to see me when I've been in need that I'm now not able to claim them in the same way that I claim my other two.

It might seem odd, but I often go for long periods without speaking to either of my friends. I grew up with one of them. Gary and I were two of six kids who skipped kindergarten and went right on to first grade. Of course we don't remember each other from those days. Kindergarteners are all so self-centered that other kids are just objects in their worlds. It's not their fault; it's just the way they are.

Anyway, Gary moved to the other side of town soon after that, and our paths didn't cross again until ninth grade. The minute we reconnected, we liked each other. We were a lot alike, and a lot different. We double-dated through high school. His girlfriend (and now wife) was my girlfriend's best friend. We liked Simon and Garfunkel's music, sports cars, and drive-in movies. Gary had a secret desire to become a doctor. I had a secret desire to be Errol Flynn in the movie *Robin Hood*. We've never really talked much about deep feelings. We've both had traumas, just like everyone else. We just know what's inside of each other. It's always seemed to have been that way. It'll probably embarrass him to even read any of this, but so what?

Twenty-five or so years ago, Gary and his family moved to the Boston area. In fact, he lived less than five miles from me. We saw each other at least once a year and sometimes even more. It has never failed me that each time we get together, it's as if we saw each other yesterday, but a marvelous thing is added. I'm somehow transported back to 1967, where I can see myself in my father's Buick, Gary alongside, on our way to pick up our girlfriends and go to someone's house or a movie or somewhere. I can remember the excitement of anticipation, and I see the world through those eyes again. It puts me back in the cycle of time, without losing where I am: no longer a child, but able to be satisfied that that boy has gone where he couldn't imagine going, and is okay now.

My other friend is Walter. We're like those old souls who have been reincarnated together in many forms over time. We also met years ago and were separated by circumstance. In the early 1970s, he drove a school bus hired by Boston College to transport students from Cleveland Circle to the main campus. He was ideally suited to travel in loops and cycles, given that he was mostly intoxicated with the Grateful Dead's music and Boone's Farm Apple Wine. I rode that bus a hundred times. I favored cream and coffee brandy, but this didn't prevent our meetings from being cordial. We didn't even know each other's names, and it was decades later that we discovered the connection. Walter headed for Oakland on some zany spree and ended up staying a while, two years, I think. I accidentally graduated and began teaching.

Teaching led to my first marriage, which led me to the world's most benign divorce and a need for housing. After three years of a mistaken marriage, I wanted a new start. Living on my own was a financial fantasy, so I was thinking of a living situation where I could get along with my housemates but have some independence.

For those readers under the age of thirty, let me digress into history here. There was no Craigslist. There was no networking. What we had was a kind of cave painting on bulletin boards at supermarkets and other similar places. People in those days would write (or make what you call hard copies) on note cards, advertising for lost cats, rides to New York for Thanksgiving, and roommates. It was from one of those cards that I remet Walter.

I found a room in a lovely house in which Walter had formerly lived, but had moved out to get married. I and three other nice but detached adults came and went as we wished, occasionally with each other and often on our own. It was probably the most civilized and graceful living situation I've encountered in my life.

Before leaving, Walter had started a garden. Like most things he did, it wasn't an ordinary garden, but an indescribably elaborate maze of mounds, flying buttresses, Incan irrigation terraces, and god knows what else. Despite the simple-to-follow instructions for its maintenance that he left behind—volumes one, two, and three—it was doomed to fail without his continued intervention.

Walter's leaving had resulted in no bad feelings. I picture his moving out kind of like a Viking funeral. I'm sure he was toasted, with everyone standing in the driveway as he and his dump truck de jour smoked on down the road. As a result, his frequent returns to tend the garden were welcome affairs. On a summer afternoon, in one of those aluminum-framed lawn chairs with the frayed plastic strips, Walter and I became reconnected.

Like Gary and I, Walter and I are very alike and very different. We both were raised as good Catholics, which is to say that we spent our early years in terror. We each had a loving but overbearing parent (my father, his mother). We each had a younger sister and the subsequent need to be left alone that only that relationship can spark. Each of us was thought to be very smart through high school, and each of us turned that around when we discovered the joys of alcohol and agnosticism in Catholic colleges.

On the other hand, I'm more planner than doer, and Walter is the opposite. I take immense pleasure in thinking about how a thing can be done, why it should be done, who would be best to do it, in what season can it be done optimally, and so on. By the time I've finished the plan for something, it's out of style.

Walter, however, frequently finds himself in the middle of a thing he's started doing—and now what? I remember the first time I visited him at his home. He lives in a modest, two-family house in a solid middle-class neighborhood. To look at the front of his house, you'd think it was a typical well-cared-for blue-collar dwelling, with maybe a grill and picnic table in the back. A peek around the corner was like looking at Mr. Myagi's Zen garden. Years of boulders picked up on landscaping sites were pieced into a four-foot retaining wall. A thirty-foot redwood tree (the kind that can't grow on the East Coast) was overhanging the three-story spiral staircase that led through the decks on the back side of the house. A thousand tulips were blooming at the foot of the shadowbox fence he made from old telephone poles and salvaged lumber.

More ominously, the wrought-iron railing for his first floor tenant's back door had been crushed flat. In the midst of the rest of the perfect yard, I had to know where this blot came from. "Oh, well, I cut down a thirty-inch wide ash tree last week, and it hit the rail." A thirty-inch wide ash tree is also pretty tall.

Walter's yard was beautiful, but not so big. The neighbors' yards were all within a few feet of each other. I had to ask. "Walter, you cut down a thirty-inch wide ash tree? Wasn't that risky?" This, of course, was a pretty safe speculation on my part, especially since I could see the rail that had been crushed.

"Yeah, well, I wrapped some ropes around it as close to the top as I could get and tied them to the telephone pole. I figured that when it started to fall, it would sort of swing around, see, kind of over here between the house and the cars. I was close to right about that, too." Close to right meant nearly knocking down the north corner of his house.

"Walter, did you do this by yourself?"

"Yeah, I was just thinking it oughta get done, you know, and I'd just oiled the chainsaw. The wife wasn't home to help, so I just kinda did it." For Walter, the wife not being home to help really means that his lovely wife, the high school guidance counselor, wasn't there to give him that look she gives him just before he starts to bulldoze the yard or cut a hole in the third-floor wall to bring in a sheet of plywood.

Walter was around when I buried my father, and I tried to be there when he buried his. He's the godfather of both of my kids and the man I'd want to have raise them if I couldn't do it myself. Through the years, Walter has helped me to be more spontaneous, to actually get more done. We've gotten old together, growing rings around our middles like thirty-inch wide ash trees. I hope I've been his friend, and I hope I've given his wife a break by keeping him off ladders and away from heavy equipment.

Island Hopping

Near the end of World War II, President Truman was faced with a decision. The future was bleak for the Japanese. They had no chance of winning the empire they had set out to gain; in fact, they were about to lose the war to the Allies. There wasn't much drama left regarding that question, but there was significant drama left surrounding the decision of how they would lose. They controlled a constellation of islands across the South Pacific, were dug in to these islands, and had determined troops ready to die defending them.

Truman's decision had to do with the use of the atom bomb. We could "island hop," making beachheads onto defended territory, fighting our way ashore, and ultimately winning, but at a cost of many Allied lives. Dropping the bomb would send the message that we could and would annihilate mainland Japan city by city, negating the need to endure many smaller battles.

As usual, there were complicating factors here, involving our ally and enemy, the Soviet Union. A quick defeat of Japan would preclude the U.S.S.R.'s being able to work east and take the island themselves. It would also allow us to demonstrate our power and willingness to use it.

We all know Truman's final decision. Judge him as you will, I believe that we all do our best, and I'll settle for that.

The idea of island hopping, though, has considerably more mileage to it than Truman's choice. It really is a useful way to view how life really is. Most of the time, we're kind of coasting on more or less navigable seas. Sometimes the waves are choppy, and we have to work a little harder than normal, and sometimes the sea is smooth as glass, and we can enjoy the sunset with a cold drink in our hands. These periods can go on long enough for us to forget that there are islands to conquer, and there most certainly will come the necessity for bloody beachheads.

My son is getting married. He's met a lovely girl. They have courted, bumped around together, and decided to tie the knot. Being a naïve romantic, he sprung the trap on her in Saint Mark's Square in Venice. He made an excuse for her to turn around for a moment, and when she turned back, he was one on knee with an engagement ring in his hand. People clapped, pigeons circled, she cried, and the deed was done. Or was it? Like many things in life, it was really only a step in a much larger dance. Now that they were engaged, they had to make wedding plans.

At this point, let me digress. I've been married twice. My first marriage was a mistake made by two nice young people, who had no business having coffee together, let alone committing to marriage. The process was probably inevitable, given the fact that I was more of an idiot then than I am now—and that's saying something. Our marriage just seemed to be a logical next step in a relationship that had to go on or break up. You don't win every coin toss.

Anyway, it was a fruitful experience for me, and I hope for my ex, a three-year crash course in self-awareness that has left no scar that I didn't need or deserve. Here's what I learned. Weddings (and other similar rituals) are intended to force decisions about what will be important to the couple when married, as opposed to what their respective families think is important. This process is often subtle, and always a little absurd. For my ex and me, it was illustrated by a bus.

My parents were practical people. They had to drive from northern Connecticut to Westchester County New York and back on a Sunday in June. Our wedding was small by their standards, only fifty people. They had about twenty of their closest friends in attendance, and they had an idea. They wanted to charter a bus. They could all ride together, sing songs, play party games, whatever. To them, it was no muss, no fuss, just leave the driving to us.

My wife had a very different vision of the affair. She had planned a graceful ceremony overlooking the Hudson River, elegant dining, sophisticated music, and a classy exit through the parking lot and on to Martha's Vineyard and our future together. No busses were included in this fantasy. Personally, I couldn't have cared less about my parents' means of getting to the restaurant at which we were to be wed. Actually, I'd ridden lots of busses, and they were okay with me.

It wasn't our first fight, but it was a classic. In the end, I had to say no to the Greyhound. I told my mother the news, and she registered mild surprise, but no more. My mother is that way. You have a better chance of deciphering eroded glyphs written by a dyslexic Mayan than knowing what my mother really thinks about something. The issue didn't return until years later when I broke the news of my impending divorce. Given my ex's intransigence about the bus, it was a miracle that the marriage lasted as long as it did.

Anyway, my son and his fiancé are making wedding plans. Details are rising up like cobras from a basket. They are trying to reconcile what they would like for their experience with what their families would like for theirs. It's one of those islands in life where bloody beachheads are the norm. In this case, of course, you have lovely people with the best of intentions, but they are under great strain due to the import of the day.

The color of the envelopes for the invitations becomes the Most Important Thing Ever, until they have to decide on the cake. Can you have carrot cake at a wedding? It's certainly nontraditional. Certain people may not like carrot cake. Are these certain people willing to sacrifice a free dessert for the good of the loving couple? Can the loving couple think of a way to accommodate this cake controversy? What about cupcakes? And so on and so on and so on.

Sane people will return to stability once the island is conquered. The wedding cake or the bus in the parking lot will subside back to the proportions they deserve. A new equilibrium will be reached. Life aboard ship will seem normal—and then another island.

This is the truth I've learned: These islands aren't the exceptions in life. The moments that loom up on our horizons as volcanic islands in our tranquil sea are as much part of things as the everyday. It's delusional to think that once the next one is overcome, there will never be another crisis. We conquered Japan, and then we had Korea. If you take the disaster de jour as all-important, you miss out on the fact that the sea is still all around you, and the sun is still setting. Do what you have to do, and remember that it will never be enough. So why nuke yourself in the process?

Sharing the Sandbox

Children's play develops as they grow up. Young kids are basically all alone in the universe. Their needs are paramount, and their play is solitary. They may include others as they do it, but the others are kind of objects in the process. After a while, they go to parallel play. I think of this as when two kids are playing at the same time and in the same place. They may even be playing the same thing, but they aren't playing with each other. Eventually, cooperative play emerges, and off we go into the social world.

Marriages are in the same categories. Marcie and I are really opposites. She expands and I contract. She's out there, and I'm in here. The things she likes are often the things I find stressful, and the things I like, she finds boring. On the surface, this would seem like a recipe for disaster, and in fact, sometimes it is. We can fight. I'm not proud of it, but we can go Hagler-Hearns with the best of them.

It hasn't always been this way. When we started going with each other, anything either of us did just seemed like the most charming thing ever. She seemed so brave, with her marathon running, dance classes, and collection of fascinating friends. I was profound and wise. My intellect was dizzying. I began to work out, and she introduced me to her professor mother. It seemed like we were converging into some uber-relationship where each of us would absorb the good from the other and probably end up on the cover of *People* magazine.

Like many things in life, after a while, the luster began to dull a little, and that's when reality sets in. Marcie is messy. She leaves things around. I don't mean a little messy, I mean MESSY. She lives life in big gulps, taking in lots of territory, moving fast and far. Along the way, shoes get left on the stairs and dishes build up in the bedroom. Her car fills up with lawn chairs and newspapers, cups with an inch of water from last week's melted iced tea, and broken earrings. Her glasses get lost and her keys are at work. In her gym bag, you could find tickets to a Red Sox game, a diamond ring, and two cans of tomatoes.

Around Marcie, I'm frequently reminded of those documentary films of sharks eating. They tear off great hunks of meat, while the water around them becomes full of enough slivers to feed a thousand smaller fish.

I tried to teach her to be more orderly. I made schedules for cleaning. I politely pointed out how easy it would be to put away things immediately after use. To provide inspiration, I helpfully reminded her of the neatness of my mother's house. No dice. My next move was humor. I put errant shoes on the mantle, in the refrigerator, under her pillow, and in dozens of other funny places. For a while, she laughed at these gestures, but at no point did any change result. Slowly it dawned on me that she just wasn't going to clean up her act.

This pattern wasn't a one-way street. Marcie wanted me to do things too. She wanted to go out more than once a month. She wanted to go grocery shopping to buy the things she wanted, even when the things I wanted were more healthful and cheaper. She wanted our kids to have friends, and so she signed them up for activities. The woman even believed in going to the doctor, something that Sicilians know to be foolish and expensive. I could see that it was going to be a long road to educate her.

The whole package became much more difficult when we had kids. Suddenly there were a million points of conflict. Marcie seemed to think that just by being their mother, she had the right to make decisions for our kids—and, wow, did we come at the decisions of parenting from different camps.

My parents were old school. There was black and white, right and wrong. Right was whatever my parents told you it was, and wrong was everything else. In my childhood, kids lived around the edges left by their moms and dads. We could watch what we wanted on television until our father was home, and then the set was his. We could play in the living room until the grown-ups came in, and then we went to the cellar or outside to play. Our free time was our own, just as soon as we mowed the lawn, put out the trash, weeded the shrubs, raked the leaves, shoveled the driveway, finished our homework, and delivered our papers.

For Marcie, things were different, very different. Her model of parenting centers on parents as facilitators. Parents exist to make a path for their kids. In her world, parents could watch television until the kids finished coloring some new masterpiece, and then all watching stopped in order to deliver proper praise and attention. The living room was open for adults until the next educational cartoon came on, and then it was time for them to leave the room to allow the kids space for free exchange of ideas. Adult free time was their own, once all lessons, games, and practices were attended, homework projects involving the recreation of the Taj Mahal were completed, application forms for horseback riding camps were filled out, and the kids were driven through their paper routes.

We had never anticipated these differences of opinions, because the values driving them were so integral to each of us that we didn't even realize they were there. Childless couples can put up with a few ladies' shoes out of place or a husband whose idea of a vacation is sitting on the other end of the couch, but throw in a kid or two, and suddenly murder seems much less implausible than before. Kids just provide so many points of contact, so many moments when choices have to be made, that all assumptions get examined and all values get tested.

Our kids have survived their upbringing, and our marriage has survived our kids. The bottom line has been that even people with huge differences can have enough in common to get by. The answer has sort of settled in around the level of parallel play. Despite my focus on the things Marcie doesn't do well, there are many necessary things that she does very well indeed, and many of these things are things that I hate doing.

I hate paying the bills. I've done it, and I think I could do it again if needed, but who would do it if they didn't have to? Marcie does it. It suits her the way she's geared to respond in the moment and meets her needs to know where we are with regard to money. Marcie also makes almost all of our social arrangements. I get included somewhere near the end of the planning process. I've learned that I get a pretty clear ratio of excuses to acceptances, and if I stick to it, things are okay.

Marcie gets the domestic mother she never had. I like to cook. I keep an eye on the home tasks like feeding the dogs and cleaning up the occasional disaster they create. I jump-start cars that have been left on all night, and I start fires in the woodstove. I watch kids when she goes to committee meetings and back-to-school nights. For me, these are usually no big thing, but for Marcie, it means that she can have friends drop in without worrying about finding the freezer frozen solid, with one box of peas suspended in the middle.

The bottom line is that some marriages are made by people who are so in tune with each other that they live their lives seamlessly. They have no conflicts or differences because they want the same things in the same amounts and ways. Marcie and I are opposites. We've had plenty of seams in our relationship—fights in the sandbox, if you will. She wanted to build bridges while I dug tunnels. The funny thing is that once we realized the value of each, we've been able to do pretty well.

Ours isn't an unexamined marriage. Neither of us is one hundred percent right about anything, but the blending of our positions—the combinations of our tunnels and bridges—has made a pretty rich and interesting life.

Justifiable Homicide

I've heard that half the marriages in the United States end in divorce. I think this is a tribute to exceptional parenting and a solid legal system. Marriage as we think of it is a terribly difficult thing to sustain. In some societies, they think our way of doing it is insane, and they may have a point.

There's an African tribe that practices a modified version of marriage that might be worth looking into. In this tribe, they marry as we do and remain monogamous. They just don't try to live together. The men maintain a communal hut, where they do men things with other men, and the women do the same with other women. Along with these communal dwellings, they maintain other smaller huts that are used when a married couple wants to spend time together. When presented with our method of marriage, they politely shake their heads and walk away.

In many parts of the world, and even in many of our own pasts, arranged marriages were the thing. The idea of choosing our own partners seems ridiculous. In our society, we think that love should be a component of the selection process. That's one of the parts of our method that really raises eyebrows. Anyone in their right mind should know that decisions made in the heat of emotion are dangerous. A cooler head is considered an asset in the spousal selection process. Your family has your best interests in mind and often knows you better than you know yourself. There's also the added incentive of not wanting to embarrass your family by failing in a marriage that they arrange.

Fifty Steps

A hundred or so years ago, divorce wasn't as necessary—at least for men. A wife was more or less chattel, a useful pet as well as a partner. At one time, a wife's assets when she entered the marriage became the property of the husband and went with him in the unlikely event of divorce. Now, I'm sure that women had power in many situations, and some of them controlled their husbands, but there was much less institutional equity. Why would there be; they couldn't even vote.

That changed around the time of the Great War(s), when men went away for extended periods, and there was nothing to do about it but let women work in factories and pay the bills. Not surprisingly, the delicate flowers did just about as well as the men, and there was no turning back. One minute they were wearing fashions that made their behinds look like the tail end of a 1966 Buick, and the next they were driving cars and drinking in public. One of the great songs of World War I was "How You Gonna Keep 'Em Down on the Farm, After They've Seen Paree?" It probably should have been "How You Gonna Get 'Em Under Your Thumb, After They Got Away?"

We men, in our infinite, blissful ignorance, thought we could just come home and keep things as they were. Women had been so placid before. They led us to believe that they liked doing what we wanted.

John Brown, the famous abolitionist, had two wives. The first (perhaps wisely) died; the second was only sixteen years old. Between them, he fathered twenty children, whom he beat regularly. He moved his family dozens of times as he started and failed in as many businesses. At least twice, he ran tanneries, the smelliest, dirtiest toxic job you'd ever need to imagine, and John Brown wasn't known for his excessive bathing. Yet he stayed married.

As for today, I can't remotely picture my wife packing and moving our two kids to go to the backyard, let alone back and forth across the wilderness. Not only was Brown a failure at most things other than impregnating his wife, along the way he used a sword to murder four of his pro-slavery neighbors and invaded a federal arsenal.

But he never got divorced.

I'm thinking in these terms because of an urge to explain—in case the worst happens and there's a murder in my home. I know that this seems over the top, and I most assuredly think that it is just that, but at the same time, we're always reading about that nice man who lived across the street who no one ever suspected would go crazy and... Well, you know the story. My guess is that the nice man (or woman, this is the twenty-first century), wouldn't ever have suspected his or her own potential either. It could be any of us.

Let me explain. I do the laundry in our house. This is really a pretty good gig, because Marcie does the bills, travel, arrangements, social planning, telephoning/emailing/general communicating with all but two or three members of the outside world, and so on. A good example of this came to light a few weeks ago on my bowling night. I was complaining about an astronomical phone bill caused by my daughter and wife. My daughter is in South Africa, a long-distance call from where we live. The bill came to six hundred dollars. I checked the message units. Marcie had 750 minutes, Julie had over eight hundred, and I had fifteen. I explained this to my bowling buddy, who asked me who I'd talked to for fifteen minutes. I had no idea I'd spent so much time on the phone.

Anyway, laundry is one of my jobs, and it sets the stage for my desire to explain, just in case...well, you know. For thirty years, every item of clothing my wife has put into our hamper has been inside out. *Every* item. I wash, dry, and fold, and I have to turn every item of her clothing right-side out before my job is done. Some of her clothes have pleats and darts and overlays and other things without names that make turning right-side out more complicated. It's not a big thing, but over years of laundry, it can begin to have an impact.

There are other things like this, such as the spoon/fork/glass that's always on the table in the den. I do dishes. I like it when they're all done. I feel proud and satisfied when they're in the drying rack, clear proof of my diligence and prowess. And then there's the spoon/fork glass to mar my perfection. No big deal, but, well, I'm just saying.

And the phone is on my side of the bed. *My* side. When it rings, I have to answer it and inevitably give it to Marcie. No one would call me; I don't talk outside of work. And I have to hand it to her so that she can check messages or call her friend Carol to find out what she wore to work on Tuesday, December 6, 1987. A little inconvenience for sure, but with the inside-out clothes, fork/spoon/glass, etc., well, things happen.

The real reason that this is all coming out now has to do with another one of those injustices of everyday living that happened on Sunday. I went bowling, as I do every Sunday. Marcie went along as she does once in a while, ostensibly to see our son (also married), who bowls with me. We got home at the same time, naturally, and she went to the downstairs big screen to watch a show she'd prerecorded. This was fine with me. It was after nine o'clock; I'd take my shower and go to sleep.

I wake up early, earlier than Marcie, so being asleep by ten fits my schedule. Sometime later, she came up. The room was dark. I was in bed. "What'cha doing?" she asked.

What'cha doing?! I'm in bed, it's probably eleven o'clock on a work night; the lights are out. What'cha think I'm doing? I'm sleeping. Or was. (By the way, how do you answer that question? If you say you're sleeping, obviously you're not, because you answered. If you don't answer, she asks again, more loudly this time, indicating that she must suspect that you're asleep because you didn't hear her the first time.)

This was a moment of truth. It must be just such moments when that nice man/woman down the street goes berserk and you read about it in the papers. What you don't read about is jury selection. If I were a defense attorney, I'd look for married jurors.

Measuring Up

I had an unsettling experience recently, one that may have been felt by others. In a way, it started when Marcie turned fifty. She is the typical wife when it comes to gifts. She doesn't want anything, but gets hurt if you don't get her anything. I'm a slow learner about relationships, but one lesson I learned in a hurry was that you always get something for her on Valentine's Day, her birthday, and your anniversary. It happens that I married a beautiful Jewish girl, so Christmas gifts are truly optional.

Anyway, it was her fiftieth birthday, and I got an idea. You see, I avoid the doctor unless I experience arterial bleeding, a protruding bone, or an inability to breathe for more than forty seconds. Marcie, of course, finds this to be just to the far side of idiotic and has told me this a thousand times. My gift was an appointment with a doctor for a physical. And that's more or less when it started.

There are few things as humbling and undignified as any kind of physical examination. For three-quarters of an hour, you are reintroduced to the fact that you're a complex machine made of meat, and you're becoming increasingly inefficient. My doctor is about as good as any, I guess, just a little younger than me, smart enough, and with the correct blend of dispassion and humor.

We've had to develop our relationship, of course. Our first meeting was like the early rounds of a boxing match. We each poked around a bit, trying to get a sense of the other. He struck the first solid shot when he told me I weighed 225 pounds. I knew I was pudgy, but 225 was a revelation.

"No I don't." I told him.

"Yes you do." he said, lightly brushing off my weak counterpunch. If he'd followed up with any kind of shot, I'd have been in trouble. Then he adds, "And at your age, that's not good. You should try to lose five pounds."

Five pounds? Five? Here's where I landed a knockdown punch. "I weigh 225, and you want me to go down to 220? Five pounds?" I've heard that a fighter knows when he's landed a telling blow, even if his opponent tries to hide it. I'm inclined to believe that, given what happened next.

He sort of stammered and said, "Well, yes. Maybe you should avoid cheese."

Cheese? Clearly he was "on queer street," unmanned by my willingness to go toe-to-toe with him. Now he and I have a different kind of conversation. He seems to know that I know my body well enough, and I know that he knows the medicine that's important to me, and I see to it that I listen to it.

It wasn't really the doctor part of the examination that threw me. That came just after, in a quite unexpected way. After the examination, you have to go to the lab to have your fluids checked. I signed in, read the paper while waiting to be called, and went in dutifully. An efficient, pleasant enough woman sat me down, wrapped my arm with rubber tubing, and drew blood. I'm not a fan of having blood drawn, or any other kind of puncture. I deal with it without too much anxiety by casually looking away as it's done. I know it takes only a few seconds, and the pain isn't worth stressing over. That isn't the part that unsettled me. The efficient-looking woman smiled and said I was almost done. Then she handed me a cup and pointed me toward the bathroom.

It really started with the cup. It had gradations on the outside, you know, little lines defining the milliliters filled after, well, just after. It wasn't a really big cup, not like those 7-Eleven Big Gulps or anything, more like the size of a small orange juice in a typical diner. I took it into the bathroom, and there in the wall was a stainless-steel cabinet, with a well-fitted door, on which there was a sign, "Insert specimens." I later found out that it had a corresponding door on the other side of the wall through which technicians could gather the leavings of those of us being judged. It reminded me for all the world of the Catholic confessionals of my youth.

The cup also had a paper label on the side, with a barcode that meant me on it. That's when I realized that what I put in the cup would have to be my best effort, but what constitutes a good effort in this regard? I could clearly see the gradations on the cup, but which level is thought of as normal? How much is a reasonable deposit? In my occasional rational moments, I see clearly that such issues are non-issues, but this wasn't one of those moments.

Then I thought some more. Is it considered gauche to fill the cup? Would they think I was showing off? I hate a showoff and presume that others do as well. I had no confusion about the fact that I wasn't going to put in too little. That has to be bad, but how much is the right amount? As distasteful as it is to think about, I had an idea. I would look into the little cabinet and get a glance at the competition. Just one look, and then I could produce the right amount, a little more than average, but not the most. I didn't want to be "over the top," so to speak.

I'm not proud to admit this. I can see how creepily disgusting it is. But there were no other cups behind the door. They must have been taken out immediately after being placed there. My imagination began to run. What if they had an alarm system that alerted all the technicians—and anyone else who might be behind the secret door—so they could *all* see what was left behind. Then they could peek out and actually see the person as he tried to leave in secret.

This was my state of mind when I tried to do as I was asked a few short minutes before. I decided to split the difference on the lines and try to hit the middle. Now the problem was that when you try, sometimes it gets harder to perform at your best. I just wasn't ready. Hey, how long do people usually need to finish the job? It can't be more than a couple of minutes. If they were waiting to see how much, why wouldn't they be interested in how long? I wasn't measuring up on any account that I could see.

In any case, I finally did what I guess I needed to do, because a week or so later, my doctor contacted me with results, and life goes on. I've had time to think about it, and I think I've learned something.

Even though I'm older than I once was, and I'm wiser (I hope) than I once was, I'm still vulnerable to what others think. I figure you can't live in a competitive society without some insecurity. Competition can be a very useful thing. It fosters innovation and spurs us on to make miracles.

It doesn't come without a cost though. No one always measures up, so let's get better at forgiving each other and ourselves, even if the cup is half empty.

Dolce Fa Niente

My wife Marcie is an extraordinary woman. There's very little she can't do or hasn't done. She had lunch with Margaret Meade and dinner with the Rolling Stones. She went to Woodstock at fifteen, and jazz musicians like Sun Ra and the Brecker Brothers slept on the floor of her apartment in the 1980s. She used to run with Bill Rodgers, and has run three marathons herself. She had her pick of scholarships for college, now has a master's degree in art therapy, and is a successful stockbroker. She babysat for Muhammad Ali's kids when they were small and has raised two kids of her own. (Well, I helped with that, but I did less than expected of the modern suburban father.) Of course, she's traveled the world, including a Micheneresque adventure across Europe in her early twenties.

It sounds like Marcie can do anything, but she can't. She can't do nothing. In Italian, there is an expression: *dolce fa niente*, it's sweet to do nothing. I personally couldn't agree more. In fact, I believe that for most of us, it's a lost art, and I don't just mean a lost art the way I've forgotten the macramé I learned in the seventies. I mean a valuable and important skill for living. It seems to me that we've come to feel that all time should be filled up with some kind of action. If we're not sweating or learning, we get vague feelings of guilt and anxiety.

The closest most of us come to doing nothing these days is when we sit ourselves down in the presence of an array of electronics and earnestly undertake the task of "unwinding." Marcie and I make it a point to watch *American Idol* every Tuesday and Wednesday. I'm not proud of that. I know that most of the people I'd like to impress just lost a great deal of respect for me, but this writing constitutes a kind of soul baring, so I'm being honest. Anyway, while watching our show, she sits with her laptop, paying bills, "friending" thousands on Facebook, and talking on the phone. During commercials, she feeds the dogs, reads, and gets in a quick shower. Tough nights are those when her beloved Red Sox are on at the same time as *Idol*. We're working on the picture-in-picture option on our cable service, but we're just too tired to get it done.

It's come to feel as though this is inherent to the human condition, but I don't believe it. My grandfather used to sit so still that birds would land on him. He was born in 1876 and spent most of his life on farms or some other way connected to the land. He fished or hunted nearly every day of his life, and he died at ninety-two.

He became a widower early, and while he continued to work to support his younger children (there were ten in all), he lived mostly alone. He spent decades in a small cabin on his brother's land, often not talking to people for months at a time. One spring, a crew inspecting the power lines that ran through my great uncles land came across the body of a man who had apparently died in the winter. They approached my grandfather and asked if he'd seen him there. My grandfather said he'd seen him, but since the man was minding his business, he decided he'd mind his too, so he had said nothing about it.

Now, I guess it isn't exactly accurate to say that farming and fishing and living off the land is doing nothing. Okay, it's more than not exactly accurate; it's full of vital jobs. But he did nothing that wasn't necessary or pleasant for him. There was very little extra noise in my grandfather's life.

In his later years, he lived with my family. Our home wasn't huge, but he could go days without really being present in the chaos of everyday life. He continued to hunt and fish. He read a book a day (he was partial to western novels and murder mysteries.), came out of his room to watch *Perry Mason* and *The Kate Smith Show*, and mostly chuckled at my sister and me.

There's a valuable lesson for parents to learn here. Work on important things until you're tired, and then shut it down. On the surface, this seems to be pretty risky. What about getting ahead? What kind of parents would let their kids veg out when the other kids are getting enriched by the minute? There are tennis lessons to help with college admissions, cello practice (Marcie tried this, but even she couldn't make it work), chess club, Scouts, karate class, yearbook, SAT tutoring, ceramics workshop, and intramural volleyball.

What we fail to recognize is the sweetness of doing nothing. If we really look at our children, the ones who are happiest are the ones who are able to do nothing. What this really means is imagining, daydreaming (which is far from wasting time), and exploring the world and themselves. The tasks of childhood aren't what we've come to think they are. We all need more nothing. It will take us time to learn how to do it. Perhaps someone will start a class for it: "Tuesdays and Thursdays, Do Nothing with Vin," a black belt in fa niente.

Wallpaper

Sometimes, parts of your life become so familiar that you don't notice they're there. It isn't important that these things are vital or trivial; they just fade into the white noise of normal, and so become forgotten in plain sight. These things can come back to you in other times, and then you remember them as if they were new. These memories can tumble one on another in a chain of associations.

The smell of new leather takes me back to when my grandfather came to live with us. I must have been nine or ten. He took over my room beside the bathroom, and I moved into the den. It was a win-win on lots of levels. Grampa got quiet and an easy walk to the toilet at night, and I got wall-to-wall bookshelves, a fireplace, and a foldout couch.

A few months ago, I visited my mother in our old home. I went into the bedroom my grandfather took over and where he eventually died, and I noticed a particular swirl in the ceiling. It was in the plaster over the spot where I lay at night. Suddenly I was five again and trying to sleep without my stuffed animals. My parents had told me it was time I went to bed without them, and although I hadn't realized that there was a time limit on such things, I accepted it. Alone in my big bed, that swirl looked like a friendly cowboy's face to me. He was there every night, and I never had to outgrow him. I never told anyone about this. It wasn't a secret, but it just wasn't anything anyone else needed to know.

Recently my daughter bought me a hat. I was tickled to realize that she thought I was cool enough to consider a racier look. I wore it around the house a little, and I even put it on once when we had friends over for a cookout, but I'm not sure it'll stick. My father wore hats. His weren't the kind fathers might wear today—no baseball caps or bucket hats, but broad-brimmed felt hats, carefully stored in oval boxes until the moment was right. These were hats that George Raft would have been proud of—no funny little feathers. He would stand by the mirror and painstakingly fold the brim over one eye. My mother hated these hats, being innately aware of fashion, but she had nothing to say about this particular statement of Dad's.

The same was true of his mustache, which was thin from the corners of his mouth to that little trough that runs down from the center of your nose. Here it rose up like two wings. I remember being small enough to be on the toilet while he trimmed it, intent on maintaining perfect symmetry. He used a small pair of scissors that he kept on a nail in the medicine cabinet. Those scissors were ridiculously delicate in his long, thick fingers. Just after he made his final self-inspection, he remembered me sitting there. He showed me how to put on shaving cream by slathering it on my cheeks and telling me who knows what. I wasn't listening to his words. I was looking forward to my own mustache. When was the last time I thought of that?

My wife has a Yankee Swap party every Christmas. She and a couple of her friends make a big deal of it, coming up with a theme, decorating, guest lists, the whole bit. Fifteen women who see each other probably twice a week, stressing about a night of eating casseroles and trading gag gifts.

My mother used to play cards with four neighborhood ladies every Wednesday night. They rotated going to each other's houses, sitting at folding tables for a few hours and talking about whatever gossip they hadn't already gone over earlier in the day. All these ladies ("the girls" my mother called them) lived within two hundred yards of each other. They saw each other every day. Many of their husbands grew up together, and all of us kids were in and out of each of their homes every day. But on every fourth Wednesday, my mother got as nervous as a new bride, unfolding the legs on the card table, making who-knows-what for them to eat while they played high-low-jack for the evening.

Wallpaper, things long forgotten that return unexpectedly. Things you bump into on the street, and suddenly you're back on familiar ground.

Yalta

In February of 1945, the Big Three met in the Crimea at Yalta to discuss the future of the world. Hitler was done, and Japan was following soon. The black-and-white photos show the three men seated: Churchill on the left, wearing a heavy, double-breasted storm coat, FDR in the center, looking worn, and a scowling Stalin on the right, hands folded across his midsection. These men were not only about to shape the future, they had plenty of history between them as well. Stalin's had a well-earned reputation for ruthlessness, and he had other reasons to be wary.

Smiling Churchill had shown a willingness to be ruthless himself as early as World War I. As a high official of the British Navy, he allowed the Lusitania to taunt the German blockade of Europe, by carrying military supplies along with their paying passengers. He knew that if the Germans sunk the ship, as they'd literally advertised they would do, then the United States would be hard pressed to avoid entering the war on the British side. One torpedo by a German submarine whose other military triumph had been a ship carrying bacon, and the Yanks were going "Over There."

Stalin remembered also that the U.S.S.R. had been squeezed by the British and the French in the run up to World War II. Many look at Neville Chamberlain's Policy of Appeasement and think that he was a deluded fool, but Stalin suspected otherwise. He thought that Britain and France had hoped that the U.S.S.R. would be attacked by Hitler. When they had sufficiently weakened one another, the major Western nations could deal with the wounded winner. It was win-win for them in Stalin's eyes.

FDR is in the middle of the photo. The man was sick, doomed to die within months, but when you look at the picture, you know that his face belongs where it is as much as the faces on Mount Rushmore belong together. The three old men sit, each thinking of how best to gain his own goals, and each knowing that compromise is necessary when it comes to deciding the future of the world.

It's hard to say what they would think about the way things have turned out so far, but lately I've been thinking about another Big Three: the Big Three of marriage. Recently I ran into a mentor of mine, who I hadn't seen in decades. We caught up on her grandchildren and my kids, and I asked about her husband. She told me he was well enough for his age and that they were still happy together. She told me that although they had their share of ups and downs, they were always together on the Big Three: sex, kids, and money. Sex, kids, and money—the three things able to make or break a marriage.

As far as sex is concerned, I was raised by an Irish Catholic mother and a Sicilian father. I undress in the dark even when I'm home alone. I learned about the physical, spiritual, and psychological dangers of sex from the best source possible: nuns. I didn't go to Catholic school like all of my cousins. Despite the fact that I didn't go to Catholic school, I did go to Catechism until junior high school and Catholic Youth Organization afterward.

This is where I received my "sex ed": Just don't do it (whatever "it" is). Those who do "it" have terrible, unimaginable fates ahead of them. Blindness, hirsute palms, pimples, and insanity are just the most visible. There are other diseases, such as pregnancy, to fear. The social stigma is beyond comprehension. Boys who do "it" are just plain bad; girls who allow them to are evil, to be shunned by the tribe. They are to be remembered for their corruption for all times. But those dangers are insignificant when compared to the horrors of eternal damnation. The flames of hell burned especially hot for those who did "it." Armed with this knowledge, I went into the world.

In a nutshell, I come to this discussion at a huge disadvantage. I will say that physical compatibility is a wonderful thing. When two people achieve it, they have a Disney World to look forward to. When they don't, it's more like World War I. In other words, it can be the source of a lot of trouble if it isn't right. The good news is that needs change, and in the case of sex, it usually becomes "muted"; it doesn't go away, but it does become less important. Just as FDR in the photo is less robust than he'd been, sex becomes a less insistent factor in a good marriage; but also like him in the photo, it's not the same without it.

Next we come to kids. Once you have them, things change. Where you once were able to live together without really questioning each other's peculiarities, now everything is on the table. Kids force husband and wife to test all the assumptions and beliefs they grew up with. They have to be blended together somehow, and that process is often messy.

My parents solved the problem very simply. Whatever my father said was law. In his absence, everything my mother said was law. If both were together, my mother could speak for him, but rarely did. Kids for him were easy: you made them, they belong to you, and they do what you say. I can't say that it was as easy for my sister and me, and I know my mother had some questions about the arrangement that she never got answered.

Marcie and I have had much more stress about the "kids" part than the others. Our upbringings couldn't have been more different. She was brought up in a matriarchal, urban Jewish setting. Her family's existence was often driven by the needs of the children. Music lessons, dance classes, bar and bat mitzvahs, and summer camps were the fabric of daily life. I was raised by Sicilian and Irish parents in an absolute patriarchy. The day was divided into the part when you're father wasn't home and when he was. As soon as dad walked in, the television, conversation, and plans for the evening were his.

This was only part of the picture for us though. Both Marcie and I were brought up by parents who loved us and in their way were there for us. Education was a value for each of our families, as was a strong work ethic. Those things have had to be the bedrock of our childrearing. Where we have differences, we each have to remember that our co-parent is intelligent and has some good reason for the decisions he or she makes. When we're at our best as parents, we're listening to each other, and one of us is letting go of a personal belief in deference to the other.

We're not always at our best, however. We've had some Ali-Frasier moments in our marriage, and if we're lucky enough to live long enough, we'll have some more. Our kids seem to have survived, with a little bruising but a little more blessing. Our son is on his own, but still calls us up, and he and I are still in a bowling league together. Our daughter is nineteen and in college. She'll also be on her own soon, and Marcie and I will have the majority of the "kids" dilemma settled.

But like Stalin after Yalta, the challenge isn't going to go away immediately. He lived until 1953, menacing his own people and the world. Our kids will continue to unintentionally cause Marcie and me to question ourselves and each other. We'll probably argue about gifts to give grandchildren or what kind of pudding they provide for us in the nursing home. It's just the nature of the beast.

Money is the last of the Big Three. Marcie and I have been much luckier than most in this regard, but still we have felt it tugging us in different directions. In the bosom of my oddly sheltered childhood, I never worried about money. At times we had none, but I was too young to remember it. My parents always worked, and we always had what I considered the best of what anyone needed. I just didn't know what anyone else felt they needed.

In our town, we were solidly middle class, and that was when middle class was really in the middle. We had a car for home and one for the store, so that made us a two-car family. We got a color television. We had air-conditioning in our living room, and once my mother took my sister and me along with another mom and her two kids, and we went for a week to the beach in Rhode Island. It was a miserable trip, remarkable only for the fact that there was an outdoor wrestling show there, and I was able to see the legendary Haystacks Calhoon, the 601-pound Country Boy from Morgan's Corner, Arkansas.

Marcie's family was also solidly middle class, but a different middle class. In Philadelphia and in South Jersey, families went away in summer to the Catskills or Atlantic City. Moms and dads took winter vacations in Cuba. Families went to restaurants regularly, and they even paid someone else to do repairs on their houses. This means that

Marcie sometimes has to remind me that a vacation to another part of the couch isn't sufficient for her. When our swimming pool needed repair, I saw it as a chance to fill the whole thing in and save the money needed to fix it. My idea of a big expenditure is to fill the tank with medium grade instead of regular.

We could have had more than one deal breaker when it came to money, but so far, so good. I give the credit to Marcie for this one. She does the money in our house; I do laundry, dishes, cooking, and anything else domestic that arises. I deal with the dogs and the weeding. I fix the shower door and the fuses when they blow. Marcie does the money. This keeps me enough out of the loop so that she can get the things done that I will mean to do but forget or that I don't know need to be done but will interfere with if I find out.

The thing about the money, third of the Big Three, is that it hasn't seemed to change much for us. We live in cycles of feeling comfortable financially and feeling stressed financially. We get a little behind, Marcie figures out a way to get through, and eventually we get a little ahead. Churchill was a little like this. He lived the longest of the three in the photo. He outlived FDR by twenty years and Stalin by seven. His fingers seemed to be in every significant event of much of the twentieth century—World War I and II, the creation of modern Israel, the independence of India, and on and on—always there and at the necessary center of something or other. It's been that way about us and money: always there as an issue, sometimes bringing joy and sometimes bringing stress, inevitable but not insurmountable if you stick together.

So there you go, the marriage Big Three. They have to go together like FDR, Churchill, and Stalin. One interacts with the other to shape the world to come. If you can manage to resolve them to each other, we can have peace at home and security abroad.

Detailed Instructions Not Enclosed

Nothing I ever did prepared me for parenthood. I'm not sure that there is anything that anyone can do that could do that. It might be that kids who have to care for siblings or farm kids are prepared, but I most certainly wasn't, and no one I know really was either.

I came to it late. My son, Michael, was born when I was approaching thirty-three. I was pretty settled in a job; some of my friends had kids already. My years as a teacher had me used to kids. My wife and I went to all the childbirth classes that yuppie suburbanites were supposed to go to, but I was not even close to prepared to be a father.

The experience was like a toboggan ride. I was perched atop an immense hill, and once I pushed off, there was no real control until the thing stopped, and control is a very big part of what makes me feel secure. One of the scariest parts of this was that I was very aware of the fact that I wasn't ready. I wasn't delusional about it; I was scared.

The main thing I was scared of was diapers. I knew that I would be involved in changing diapers, and the thought was more than I could take. Peepee diapers I could get used to pretty quickly, but the other kind? Well, the other kind haunted me. Before I give the wrong idea, I'm not enough of a moron to think that diapers were the most important thing to be scared of. It's just that they were the only concrete thing to which I could attach my fear.

As the big day drew close, my terror began to twist me into unexpected shapes. I was never not scared, but I became able to pretend that the actual day wasn't really coming. It was easier than it sounds. Contemporary pregnancy can be pretty surreal. I remember that we went to a doctor's appointment and saw an ultrasound picture of our son in the womb. The doctor pointed out things like legs and heartbeat, and I ooo'd and ahhh'd, but truth be told, it didn't look like any of that stuff to me. It mostly looked like the Shroud of Turin. It constitutes clear proof to true believers, but to the skeptical, who can say?

To really understand the depths of my insanity during these days, I have to explain about The Stupidest Thing I've Ever Done. In a life that so far has spanned nearly sixty years, I've done many stupid things. Most are the little stupid things that we all do and no one notices, but a fair number have been really remarkably stupid, the kind of stupid that stuns crowds, the kind of stupid that pauses time so that everyone can appreciate that they are present during a truly exceptional moment.

It happened during our last doctor's visit before our scheduled C-section delivery. We knew that the C-section would be necessary, so all we were waiting for was for the doctor to tell us the baby was ready, and we were a go. Well, we sat in the office, with the doctor facing us. She smiled and said that we could go ahead and schedule the operating room for the delivery. She went on to say that it would be available either Monday or Tuesday.

My dewy-eyed wife looked to me for guidance and support to make the call. I thought a second, and then a miraculous thing happened to me. I believe it was a kind of out-of-body experience, because I knew what I was about to say and was actually present while I heard myself say, "Well, I have my bowling league Monday night." All the while, my astral self was screaming "No! No!" but the words slipped out anyway.

The doctor's mouth slackened. Marcie gave me a look that has never been seen outside particularly bloody Civil War battlefield hospitals. It couldn't be unsaid. It was a moment in which I was in a confined space with two women who were in biblical spasms. All the atavistic horrors ever visited upon women by men had been heaped upon them at that moment, and I sat, a drooling idiot, about to be a father.

Despite my denial and incompetence, our son Michael was born. The C-section was a success, but Marcie had complications. It seemed that in the recovery room, she got hold of a glass of ginger ale. Carbonated beverages after abdominal surgery isn't fatal, but it is painful. Michael and Marcie spent their first ten days together in the hospital.

While I was quite sympathetic with my wife's suffering, the arrangement wasn't altogether bad. I got to be a father during visiting hours, sitting in a rocking chair with a hospital gown on, holding the baby. Fatherhood couldn't have been easier. What had I been worried about? Here I was, fathering like a champ, at least for a while, until the nurses took him back to the nursery. Clearly, there were a few aspects I hadn't yet faced.

Ten days of buffet parenting, and wouldn't you know it, Marcie got better. We had to leave the hospital, and not just us, we had to take the baby with us. A nurse pushed Marcie down the ramp in front of the hospital, put the baby into the car seat in the back of our car, and then the nurse left. She left! Was she crazy? Did the hospital administrator know about this colossal error? They would immediately fire the nurse for committing this surely criminal gaffe. Honking horns and grouchy valet parkers brought the grim truth to me. We were now on our own. Home we drove.

These are the times that the tribe comes together to acknowledge its good fortune. We had plenty of friends and family there when we got to our house. Mothers in good standing cooed and clucked, while the other dads and I ate casseroles. The baby slept some (but not much), and everyone rejoiced. Right after that, they left. Those were the quietest, most awesome moments ever. Just us, and us included a baby. We had no one there to help. We had no instruction manuals. We just had us, and that's one of life's most valuable lessons. There are almost no absolute rights and wrongs in child rearing. Don't hurt them, feed them what they want to eat, let them sleep if they will, hold them whenever you can, and live the life you were living as much as possible. The baby will just come along.

I knew I had turned a corner as a father about three months later. We had house guests from Michigan, and they gave us a chance to go out without Michael. We jumped at it. It would probably make me sound like a better person if I were to say that I was too anxious to enjoy my dinner, but that wasn't true. What I felt was less focused than that. I had the nagging feeling that I had forgotten something very basic to my day-to-day functioning, like maybe I wasn't wearing pants or something. It came to me that we'd had our son with us pretty much constantly since the hospital. Wearing pants isn't a burden; it's just something we do. Having the baby with us was like that.

Our daughter was born six years later. It was different, but the same. For Michael, we had tried to be ready. We had changing tables, fancy strollers, car seats that astronauts could have used safely, at least two thousand articles of clothing that were outgrown in fifteen minutes, safety locks for the garage (detached and never used by us, by the way), and lord knows what else.

When Julie was born, we went to Costco and got a case of paper towels and a hose. This might make it seem like we were more ready for the second child. I think the opposite is true. We knew that we couldn't be prepared. We would have our daughter, get to know her, and she would get to know us. Eventually, once we'd accomplished that, something new would come up, and we'd have to do it over again. That's parenthood: living your life with another smaller person along for the ride. After a while, you become smaller, and if things go well enough up to that point, you get to go along for the ride. The owners' manual gets written with the owning. Don't be frightened of that, it's been that way all along.

Revelations

My daughter and I are starting to get along. She's now nineteen and has spent a year at college. I'm fifty-nine and have spent lots of years at lots of things. It's not that we haven't always loved each other. It's not even that we haven't always been pretty proud of each other. It's just that we haven't always gotten along with each other.

Frankly, that's often been surprising to me, because I think of myself as someone who is very easy to get along with. I have a great store of wisdom that allows me to give excellent and sensitive advice. I have read many, many very deep books and so have gained lots of knowledge of weighty things. My unique upbringing and my years as a teacher have led me through the paths of the human heart and have generated in me a wealth of empathy. With all this in mind, it has always been clear to me that the difficulty we have had getting along has been a result of my daughter's immaturity, so I waited patiently (or kind of patiently) for her to come around.

The revelation I've waited for didn't come all at once. It's been a process, with steps forward and slips back, and I'm sure we'll continue on this road for the rest of our lives. I can say, though, that the first step came like a bolt of lightning.

Julie had always been a good athlete. She has unusually good eye-hand coordination and is very strong. Her competitiveness rivals grim death for its constancy and intensity. Since we live in the suburbs in the new millennium, all this has been channeled into organized team sports. She's played soccer, basketball, softball, swimming, lacrosse, hockey, and tennis. (At night, when I silently speak to whatever spirit may run the universe, I give thanks that our town doesn't have a polo team.) This has meant constant rushing to practices, lessons, games, meetings, sign-ups, and spaghetti dinners.

Through it all, there was always one constant. Julie hated to have Marcie or me at any of these events. We've had innumerable scrapes over our attendance at games, usually involving her frantically waving at us to leave the side of fields, courts, and rinks. It was simply agonizing for her to have us at games. This pattern caused us no end of grief. I'd start to calmly reason with seven-year-old Julie, explaining clearly that we cared a great deal for her and spent much of our free time driving her from place to place, and that we wanted to enjoy watching our little girl. The final result of these interactions was the realization that it's beyond stupid to try to reason with a seven-year-old, and Julie was possibly the most unreasonable seven-year-old kid ever.

From reason, I went to brute force. I insisted on going, even though this sparked epic scenes on sidelines throughout New England. Eight, nine, ten, eleven, the struggle continued. At some point in there, I began to withdraw from the fighting. This was because I thought I'd had an insight into the reason Julie was so adamantly against having her parents at her games. It hit me that she was worried that if she played poorly, she'd be embarrassed in front of her family. She didn't want us to see her fail!

With that thought, it all came together for me. The poor kid so wanted us to be proud of her, she couldn't tolerate the danger of a disappointing play. My attendance at games became less frequent, although Marcie continued to go. She's a much more social person than I, and most of the time, Julie tolerated her talking to the other moms, making car pool plans, and arguing calls.

Things continued like this for quite a while. I'd slip into a game or two now and then. Julie would see me, turn red, and mouth, "Get out!" across whatever playing field she was on. Given my clear understanding of her feelings, and not wanting to increase the tension she felt about failing in front of me, I'd pretend not to see her. I can't call it a truce, and I won't say that it satisfied either of us, but it felt like a compromise. I thought that I was doing my duty as a father to help my little girl develop healthy self-esteem.

One day, at a high school junior varsity girls' basketball game, the truth struck me like a thunderbolt. It was a Friday afternoon game, and her godfather Walter and I showed up. Julie and Walter have a special bond. No one can tease Julie or deal with her moods the way he does. I knew that she would never ever ever want to do poorly in front of him, so when she saw us in the bleachers, I was rocked when she smiled at him, waved hello to him, and then turned to me with her Medusa stare and pantomimed for me to leave.

There was a second of confusion and then a torrent of realization. My daughter wasn't afraid of embarrassing herself; she was afraid of *me* doing something embarrassing! The next wave to hit me was a refinement of the first. She wasn't afraid that I would do something embarrassing. That wasn't necessary at all. Just my existence was embarrassing to her.

I'd known teenage girls who felt this way. After all, I'd taught for nearly thirty years at the time. Those girls though had fathers who *were* embarrassing. I wasn't like that. I'm pretty cool. I dress well for my age. I rarely pick my nose when people are looking. I brush often. What could she possibly be thinking?

Later, I brought this up to Marcie. Having been a girl herself at one time, I hoped she could shed some light on the subject. Marcie wasn't at all surprised at Julie's reactions; in fact, she was mostly surprised that even a self-deluding dummy like me would have taken so long to figure it out.

Once I finally came to the truth, I had to think of what to do about it. My head began to cool, and it became clear. It wasn't really me. I'm not significantly dorkier than the other dads. It wasn't Julie. She isn't more sensitive than the average teenaged girl. I wanted to do something that would acknowledge her feelings, while letting her know mine.

Walter was consulted. At this point, it will be helpful to get an idea of Walter and me in a more visual mode. We're both kind of grizzled. I could lose forty pounds and be pretty normal. Walter has one of those midsections that can best be displayed in one of those dark T-shirts with breast pockets. After a lengthy discussion over donuts and diet root beer, our plan was decided. Julie needed a sense of proportion.

Her view of things needed to be broadened. We recognized the typical nature of her perceptions, but we also knew that Julie was an exceptional child who could grow from experience.

Our plan was as follows: We were going to paint her number (34) on our bellies, and when she was taking a foul shot, we'd both stand up and cheer, simultaneously lifting our shirts. We believed that this would give her some perspective on embarrassment. We knew that having had that experience, our normal presence would return to the mild, supportive place in which it belonged.

It has been a policy of Marcie's to interfere in Walter's and my plans. More than once she's refused to let us follow through on ideas that would have changed many things for the better. She told Julie our idea. Julie seized up with fury. I agreed to hold off, but I neglected to get a hold of Walter. He lives about twenty miles from us, right beside a town where Julie plays ball.

Walter showed up at a game, as he has done for years, and sat in the bleachers. Julie spotted him right off and began to gesture. He playfully flipped up the hem of his shirt, just a little, as a kind of joke. Julie gestured again, more flipping. At that point, Julie's coach saw that strange guy in the stands, making threats to her players. She went off and called the police. Walter is the gentlest man who ever lived, but he doesn't necessarily look that way. Fortunately, Julie caught on to what was happening when she saw the commotion in the stands. After a few tense moments, the problem was worked out. No gestures, no belly paint, no jail.

I think the experience helped Julie. She has come to realize the depths to which her dad will go to participate in her life. I think she now understands that having me at her games is a good compromise. She knows that we love her, and she has come to see that, while we're embarrassing, things could be worse.

Kodak Moments

My daughter loves Disney World. We've been there perhaps ten times. That's not to say that our trips there have always been smooth. Trips for our family are never smooth, and trips for our family with Julie usually develop into adventures. You know the kind: *Gilligan's Island*, three-hour cruise kinds of adventures. Julie just gets so excited that little glitches seem like big disappointments. And to her, disappointments are acts of aggression. Then we fall into tribal warfare.

I, on the other hand, have my own travel issues that I tend to think of as genetic. Ever since my paternal grandparents sailed to Ellis Island, voyages have been suspect. It's not always clear where you'll end up. Suffice it to say that when we vacation, things happen.

Once we went to Mexico with my wife's brother and his family. These are people I adore, and with whom I have lots of fun. They're great to travel with, because they keep my wife amused without testing the limits of my anxiety about being out of my element—usually. On this trip, I was informed that we were going to visit some Mayan ruins some miles away from our nice, safe, all-inclusive hotel. Marcie and her brother had rented a van, gotten directions from some fifteen-year-old who made beds at the resort, and were thus ready to venture into the unknown.

Our two families piled in, and we started off. The first road was kind of a highway, with police checkpoints every five miles or so. Eventually, we turned off onto a largish dirt road. Four or five miles later, this road began to narrow. It became so narrow that the anorexic dogs and goats tethered to the sides of the huts we passed could gnaw on the tires if they so desired. From there we took a left turn onto a side street. *Side street* is, of course, a euphemism for a dirt track with jungle vines groping into the open van windows.

Marcie and her brother were blissful. This was just the kind of adventure they crave. The kids were young and couldn't know that they were probably going to disappear and never be found. My sister-in-law and I were the only two who could see the disaster looming in our immediate future, but through some silent pact, we said nothing. I guess neither of us wanted to scare the innocents who were about to die.

At the end of this track, we entered a clearing. There were huts around two sides, pigs and chickens rooting around, and a dozen or so people warily eyeing us as we parked the van. I felt as if I were on a menu. It turned out that we were at the entrance to a Mayan city that had been partially excavated, I think in the 1960s, but the work had stopped when they ran out of money. There were men there who were licensed to guide people through the area. We hired one and started out.

The people in the village were actual Mayans. They didn't speak Spanish as a first language, though they did speak it, as well as English. Our guide was gracious and informative. The excavations were fascinating. The whole site had a resonance of thousands of people who had lived there, where there was now jungle.

We hiked along an overgrown Mayan road to see a pyramid about a quarter-mile away. With lush trees, ferns, and vines all around us, on a path crossed by leaf-cutter ants and indescribable butterflies, something amazing happened. Through the rainforest, wearing hats with mosquito netting, came two people. They emerged twenty feet from us, turned, and said, "Marcie, is that you?" Here in this ancient city, five thousand miles from home and twenty miles from even a Coca-Cola, were two clients my wife had spoken to less than a week earlier. It felt as though we were bumping into them at our local supermarket.

Marcie has a way of collecting people. She's interested in them, remembers their stories, and calls on their birthdays. She has no idea what "mind your own business" means. She thinks that everyone's business is her business, and she acts accordingly. Amazingly enough to me, the large majority of people see this as friendship. They love her. I've mulled this over during the past thirty years we've been together, and I've come to a few conclusions.

First, people like it when other people are interested in them. They like it when someone notices that they lost five pounds. They like to talk about their ex-husband or wife to be who is a lousy spouse, but is good to the kids. They like to shop for flower pots and peasant skirts with someone who laughs at their jokes. They like it when people are involved with them. Of course this isn't true for everyone, but for plenty of folks, it's absolute gospel.

This leads to a corollary truth that takes me back to Disney World. The last time I was there, I got an idea that would amuse Julie and that interested me in other ways. At Disney World, people take pictures. They take pictures of their kids with Cinderella, they take pictures of parades, they take pictures of their five-year-olds as they try to climb on statues of Mickey's wizard hat, they take pictures of everything. I know, because I have pictures like these in our family albums.

The thing that I found intriguing, and that Julie found amusing, was the people in the background of these pictures. In nearly every picture taken in a place like Disney World, there are strangers in the background. What I decided to do was to try to get into as many pictures as I could, without disturbing the actual people intended to be there. I slipped behind Japanese tourists. I casually wandered beside high school cheerleading squads on holiday. I inserted myself next to Chinese acrobats performing for the crowds. Julie thought it was hysterical (and I thought it was kind of funny too).

Along with the humor, though, I was thinking of something else. I was going home with these people. I would be immortalized in slide shows all over the world. My face wouldn't be noticed as I seemed to be walking randomly behind Grandma, but it would be there.

I find the combination of anonymity and intimacy fascinating. We see it all the time, but we rarely think about it. In traffic, when someone passes us, we think they're aggressive imbeciles, but when we're cruising along and the light changes, we think little of getting into the shorter line and moving ahead. We're not trying to take advantage of anyone, but that's how we feel if we're in the other car. In a restaurant, when someone's kid bumps your chair, it's easy to think that they're the unruly product of irresponsible parents, but when our kids were little, they were just so cute that no one could object to their harmless wanderings. We forget that we were there once or that we will be there sometime soon.

In our crowded world, we erase whatever it is that makes us notice other people around us, unless they do something unusual. But the people around us are just as real as those that wandered out of the Mexican jungle to say hi to my wife, just as real as I was in the background of those pictures. We have to be a little bit numb to survive the sensory overload of our busy times, but every once in a while, it's fun to get into someone else's.

Parents' Weekend

Four years ago, my son graduated from college, and now my daughter is in college. This allows me to speak with some expertise on experiences of institutions of higher learning. Every year, colleges have what they call "parents' weekend." The apostrophe can be taken to mean that the weekend is for parents—that it belongs to parents. The first time my wife and I attended one of these, that was our expectation. We were proud and earnest about it. We kind of expected to be the guests of honor (along with a couple of thousand other parents) of the institution our kid was attending and to which we were sending a healthy portion of our retirement savings.

We had received a schedule of events planned for our information and edification. Concerts given by student musicians, sporting events staged by student athletes, lectures, tours, a chance to meet the president of the school (along with a couple of thousand other parents), and so on. I expected the whole thing to be like the Thanksgiving pageants we went to when the kids were in second grade, only lots more expensive. I had vague, semi-conscious fantasies about my son in a turkey costume, making me beam with pride at the superior quality of his gobbles or at my daughter's stand-out pilgrim hat, cleverly cut out of construction paper, hanging in a place of prominence along the corridor of some ivy-covered building.

My kids both went to the same college, a three-hour drive from our home. I thought and still think that this is a good distance for kids to be away from home. It's far enough so that they get a sense of independence and close enough to get there for important moments like graduation, disciplinary hearings, and parents' weekend.

The weekend is invariably scheduled two months into the year, so that the kids are established in school and to make sure your check has cleared. It's likely that within a week of your kids having started, they either began calling home every morning at three to complain about their psychotic roommate, or they disappeared and haven't contacted you at all. Obviously, each of these scenarios have their own joys, hopefully culminating on parents' weekend, when you can meet the psycho or see your missing milk-carton kid and get to the bottom of the reality of the situation.

In any case, the first time you go, it's with anticipation and some illusions about the shape of your experience to come. This illusion is almost always completely inaccurate and inadequate. It happens that our kids' school is one of those liberal arts institutions inhabited primarily by healthy American youth whose parents must drive SUVs, have a golden retriever, and own a vacation home somewhere expensive. Consequently, the Friday evening of parents' weekend is marked by a four-mile line of Range Rovers and Lexuses (Lexi?), all jockeying for spaces in the parking lot of a nationally known hotel chain.

The experience is all the more bizarre, because no one is behaving as they would in their real lives. In my real life, I scream and grumble when I have to wait more than fifteen seconds for anything. Here, I act as though I have a direct line to the Buddha, calmly allowing someone with New York license plates to take the only available space, because he has a sticker in his window that's from the same college my daughter goes to.

When you get to within an hour or so of the school, you call from the car, excited about the honor to be bestowed upon you, and the joy your child must be experiencing because he or she is about to see you after such a long time. A discerning parent might be mildly unsettled when your phone call is greeted by an annoyed teenager, who was just about to take a shower/ go to the laundry/ eat a Ding Dong.

"We're almost there, sweetie! Only an hour away! We can't wait to see you!"

"Huh, oh, yeah, yeah."

"We'll call you as soon as we get in! It won't be long now honey! Where do you want to go for dinner?"

"Huh, oh yeah, dinner, yeah. Well, yeah, dinner."

"Honey, is everything all right? I mean, you sound kind of preoccupied."

"Huh, well, yeah, well, I was just about to take a shower/ go to the laundry/ eat a Ding Dong."

"Well, you go right ahead. We'll call you as soon as we get in. Think about where you want to eat dinner."

"Huh, yeah, okay, yeah, dinner."

Most of the time, parental fantasies sustain them through this initial warning period. We can't seem to imagine that our offspring aren't as excited to see us as we are to see them. After all, this is parents' weekend.

The next call can be even more perplexing. "We're here! We just got in and we're in the room!"

"Huh, the room? Huh?"

"You know, Cupcake, the hotel room. It's okay. Only a cot and a washbasin next to the boiler in the basement, but what can you expect? It's parents' weekend, and it was only nine hundred dollars a night, if we help empty the trash into the dumpster."

"Huh. Oh yeah, the room."

"Have you decided where you want to go for dinner? We're famished from the long ride."

"Huh, dinner? Oh yeah. Hey, my roommate and seven of the international students are going to come with us. Their parents couldn't come for the weekend. Most of them are playing in a golf tournament in Tahiti. We want to go to the Platinum Menu. It's right downtown."

"The Platinum Menu? I read about that in *Fine Dining Magazine*. Isn't that the restaurant that uses solid gold forks?"

"Huh, forks? Yeah, I think so. My roommate has never had caviar or escargot, so we want to go there."

"Uh, okay, darling, I'll call and see about a reservation for all ten of us."

"Huh, yeah, call."

By now, you should have gotten an inkling that parents' weekend is not as your half-formed fantasies suggested. Any normal person should be getting the idea that the role of the parent during parents' weekend is a little different from that of the guest of honor. Of course, dinner reservations at the Platinum Fork can only be had within fifteen minutes of your call, or at 12:30 at night. Twelve-thirty works fine for your daughter, because she won't be ready until midnight, because the Ding Dong machine in the dorm needs to be refilled and will take that long. Anyway, at 1:15, she and her friends are planning to attend a naked skinhead poetry reading at an abandoned crack house beside the railroad tracks.

Bewildered and disillusioned, you wait another six hours before you eat, barely pass the credit check run by the restaurant, and treat your daughter and her friends to a meal they hardly eat, bringing the bulk of the three thousand dollars worth of food back to their dorm in two small bags and a Dixie cup.

The next day, after a questionable night's sleep on your cot, you try again. At noon you call. "Hey, sugar, are you up?"

"Huh, wha', huh?"

"It's Mom and Dad. Are you up?"

"Huh?" Click.

Remembering your child's late night literary pursuits, you decide to call again in an hour. "Boopsie, are you up yet?"

"Huh. Up? Huh. Yeah. Hey I dreamt that you called before. Isn't that funny?"

"Yes, babycakes, hysterical. What should we do today?"

"Huh. Today? Oh yeah. Today. I need to go to the mall."

"The mall, lovemuffin? What do you need at the mall?"

"Huh, need, huh. Oh, well, boots. And two new sweaters. And I promised to pay for my friend's oil change at the Jiffy Lube. And an espresso maker. And a birthday present for the kid who lives downstairs who invited me to his birthday party and he's in the hospital now because of the accident. And a new backpack because my old one is blue and I need a green one. And some cat food for the cat that comes around sometimes. And…"

Well, by now, the thrill is gone. All illusions are shattered. It has become clear that parents' weekend means that it's the weekend your parents come and meet all the needs that have built up since they were last available. Dinners are spent by your daughter gossiping with all the new friends you're paying to feed, and breakfast (at the now unimaginable hour of 11:00 a.m., just so you can hit maximum traffic on the long ride home) is spent with a surly, overtired teen who somehow manages to find someone to text with while you try to say your good-byes.

Take a bit of advice from a veteran of many parents' weekends. See if you can find a golf tournament in Tahiti.

The ABCs

There are many questions these days about what students need to learn before they can graduate from high school. Teams of educators couple with community leaders, captains of industry and of just about every other place come together to add their input. Each is sure that they must get their point across before we turn some kid loose with a diploma that doesn't prepare him for whatever they see as the future. Engineers worry that we're falling behind the rest of the world in math. Parents who barely survived elementary school and who haven't been more than a hundred miles from home since complain that their kids don't know where Sri Lanka is on the map. Panels confer and experts debate, eventually coming up with some plan that they can't pay for and that some other panel will discredit in two years.

Okay, I know I'm being harsh. It is important that we constantly examine the education we give our children, and the things they need to know. My problem is that very few schools teach some of the most needed and useful things we encounter. Here is my list of what we should insist all children know by the time they graduate from high school:

1. *How to change a tire.* I know all about AAA. I have it and use it whenever I can. My son and daughter have it too. That doesn't mean they shouldn't be able to perform this basic task. Heaven forbid you have a flat out in the middle of nowhere. It could save hours if you can change it yourself. Possibly more important than that, though, is the feeling of confidence that comes from being able to take care of

at least some of your own troubles yourself. Too many things are too complex for us to manage these days. A little do-it-yourself is good for the soul.

2. Repairing a leaky toilet. This falls into the same category as fixing a flat, except that it's easier to live with a toilet that runs a little and wastes water. The mechanics involved are pretty simple. If you can shut off a faucet and use pliers, you can help yourself and save a bit of the planet.

3. Being able to cook at least three basic meals. When you're small, your mom cooks for you. She makes sure your hands are clean and that you eat a few vegetables along with your hot dog. By the time that you graduate from high school, you're not little anymore. Your mom can still cook most of your meals, but you should also be able to make things like pasta with simple tomato sauce, a good omelet, a broiled hamburger (or steak, piece of fish, etc.), and a couple of salads. There's no reason you can't. Maybe you don't like pasta. You'd have to be crazy not to, but it's a big world and there are crazy people in it. If you don't like it, don't make it, but you must be able to make something else that's not primarily frozen or from a can.

4. How to tell good art from bad art. There's more than a little element of subjectivity here, I know, but every kid should have been exposed to a variety of music, literature, and fine arts, and be able to know what they like in it. I'm not a big fan of certain genres of music, but someone who is should be able to tell me what there is about it that they like. Art makes a person whole. It allows us to communicate to each other on a very deep and important level. It transcends language and culture, history and belief system and just speaks from heart to heart.

5. Driving a stick shift. This may be something of a lost art. It's not as useful as it was when I first started to drive, but it still comes up now and then. My son tried to learn this on an old car I had. He was close to being able to do it, but panicked at a stop light on a hill, and that was that. His friend got him through the intersection, and he was done. Years later, he rented a car in Italy, and lo and behold, it was a stick. After his initial freak out, he got the hang of it. It's now another of those things he does that gives him confidence in himself.

6. *Being able to apologize.* This is a hard one for me. I don't have trouble apologizing for things that I don't think I'm really wrong about—for instance, your misunderstanding of what I mean by something I say—but I do have trouble when I really should be sorry. It's not the feeling of sorrow for my act that's lacking; it's the ability to be wrong that's the issue. This is a real skill to learn. It's unbelievably useful and powerful.

The first time I remember seeing the value in being sorry and saying it came several years ago. While rushing out to work one morning, I accidentally brushed my car against Marcie's. It wasn't a huge gouge, but there was a visible scratch. I chose to say nothing and hope that it would blend in with the normal dings and dents that our vehicles accumulate over the years. Marcie noticed it at the end of her workday. It was one of those workdays when you really could use something to vent about.

Her parking lot at work is small, the spaces tight to each other. She'd lived with it as much as she lives with anything, complaining to her boss now and then about the inconvenience. This was a smoking gun, and she went to town. Her boss was sufficiently chastened to notify the building manager, informing him that he may be looking to renegotiate their lease because of this problem.

Anyway, you can see where this is going. I had a moment of moral crisis when I weighed the possibilities surrounding remaining silent and speaking up, and I decided to spill my guts. It wasn't a scene riddled with pathos. I didn't snivel or break down in an unseemly manner. I did contritely come clean, admitting my error and offering my apology. To my surprise, Marcie accepted it and we moved on. Come to find out, apologizing the right way is a real time and suffering saver.

I'm sure that there are other things of this nature that you and your own panel of experts can come up with for qualification as a requirement for graduation. Likewise, there are likely to be some things on my list that aren't as important as they once were. Lord knows that I stopped paying attention to most of the things we call progress a long time ago. This means that there are certainly new things (computer technological things, for example) that should be included that I don't know, but it's too late to do anything about it now. I already have my diploma.

Paternity

Without my realizing it, my children have grown up. Of course I knew they were getting older, and I hoped I was giving them the best tools I could to cope with the world, but at the same time I knew that the world with which they'd be coping would be different from the world I knew.

It was clear to me that my parents were benignly incapable of understanding my life. I suppose that it makes sense that this is the same for my kids. Anyway, it's mainly in retrospect that I see that my parenting style has been laissez-faire. This is surprising to me, given my propensity to try to control everything in my general vicinity. When I drive somewhere unfamiliar, I want to know things like how many fire hydrants between my door and my destination and how many places there are on the way to get pancakes. Intellectually, I realize that control in this world is an illusion, but emotionally I'm happier to kid myself than face bleak reality.

Anyway, as a parent, I think I've been relatively hands-off. It's probably pretty selfish of me though. I've always liked my privacy, and kids can seriously cut into that. Soccer games and class projects can put quite a dent in Daddy's afternoon television time. I'll risk being clichéd and say that when I was a kid, my parents checked my report card, responded to all-points bulletins about me, provided a couple of meals daily, and otherwise left me alone. Oh, there were chores and obligations, but once they were discharged, I might as well have been invisible.

That was mostly a good thing, I think. I didn't bear the weight of the world if my geometry grade wasn't as good as someone else's kid's, and I was spared the burden of carrying on the family's tradition of being the best baseball player on earth. The lines were pretty clear, and predictability is probably the most important thing for most of us. I knew my parents would be there if I needed them, and so I didn't need them very much.

I would have been happy to continue in this style, but you don't get to have kids by yourself. Parenting in my world has involved negotiating with another human being who thinks she has as much to say about the whole affair as I do. It's a comfort to be able to share some responsibilities, but it also calls for compromise, not my best thing.

Anyway, it's been more than twenty-one years since our youngest was born, so we have less parenting to do. I'm not ready for the rocking chair, but I can see it on the porch through the front window. Not only that, but parenting our kids now is different from when they were little. It was embarrassing to have them tantrum in the supermarket, but when they did, we could pick them up and put them in their car seat. Nowadays, crises tend to be more critical. They happen at greater distance and involve more important things.

There's also the curse of unwanted wisdom to factor in. I'm old enough to see where my kids are in danger of making mistakes, but I have less to say or do to help them avoid them. On my better days I can acknowledge that making mistakes, realizing them, and doing the repairs is really only living your life. There are probably as many errors as triumphs to experience, and as someone must have said some time ago, you grow more from problems than solutions.

The bottom line is that I'd feel better if every day of my kids' lives were filled with Disney butterflies in Bambi's forest—before the shooting, that is. Of course that will never be the case, and I've had to come to grips with keeping my mouth shut, even (maybe especially?) when I know better.

So what brings this to mind today? This time it's Julie. Julie, my challenging, delightful, infuriating, interesting, etc. etc. etc. daughter. She is finishing her junior year in college and is doing it abroad. In my conservative dad fashion, I tried to point out that Canada is abroad, as are other familiar and (supposedly) civilized countries like England and Vermont. Why not go somewhere like that, where I can predict that things will be safe, where there are few if any poisonous snakes, and I could come to the rescue if needed? Not my Julie. She's in South Africa.

Now, before I get ahead of myself and say things that are insulting, let me seriously explain how I feel about South Africa. It's a beautiful place. The people there have a spotty history, but so does the United States and every other country in the world. I get a sense from Julie that there's change going on, learning and adapting to a new kind of society, opportunities to learn from the past and forge a new future, but it's just so far away! So far away and so *different*. I'm never too far from worry about her getting into trouble and being out of my reach.

Okay, no one has to tell me how pathetic I sound. Leave me alone.

So what happened? Marcie went to South Africa a few weeks ago and spent time with Julie. It was a nice trip, with only one mother-daughter argument and plenty of sightseeing. It goes without saying that Marcie got to the bottom of every detail of Julie's social life on the Dark Continent. Her report was almost completely favorable. She has good and interesting friends, plenty of things to do, and plenty of places to go.

And she has boyfriends. This has been an issue for us, because Julie can be hard on people. Did I say hard on people? Julie can roar like a forest fire and hit like a train. She is the best friend and worst enemy you can have, and she's often so in less than five minutes. In high school, there seemed to be few boys who interested her. In college we couldn't really tell, and she wasn't about to call up and let us know. In Africa it was impossible to avoid getting the details, and Marcie wasn't trying to avoid them in any case.

Phone calls from South Africa are ridiculously expensive, so Marcie and I spoke perhaps three times in the two weeks she was there. This was probably good, given that the first time she called she told me that a young man had offered ten cows for Julie's hand in marriage. I didn't quite know how to take that. Is that a good price? Was Julie being complimented? And what kind of cows are we talking about? Are they those skinny-looking cows you see on Discovery Channel that look as though they could fight off a lion if they had to, or nice black-and-white milk cows, or maybe even fat, placid beef cattle? That could mean a lot of steaks.

Ultimately it didn't come to anything. Marcie overplayed her hand and asked for twenty. To her it was an exercise in negotiation more than an actual opportunity. Even with our permission, he had no chance with Julie, and it wouldn't be fair to take his herd and leave him empty-handed. It turns out that he didn't have twenty head, but he agreed that it would be a fairer price. I hope Marcie's counteroffer didn't hurt his feelings. Besides, Julie liked a young man named Lionel more.

Lionel is a tall, handsome senior economics student. He speaks with a British accent and holds doors open. According to Marcie, he's clearly well-bred and has good prospects. None of this matters to me; I want her to come home, and if she must marry, it should be to someone like...well, I don't really know what he should be like, but he should at least be from nearby.

No worries though, as of our last call from Julie, Lionel is out of the picture. Marcie asked her how Lionel was doing, and she said, "Lionel. I'm done with Lionel."

"Why? What happened?"

"He lied to me. I'm done with him." Marcie, wanting to be the consoling mother asked what he lied about. "He told me he was poor! He's not poor! His father owns a corporation in Johannesburg, and his mother is a doctor!"

Huh? What's a father to say? Be careful, and we'll see you in June.

BFF

Who are these people who want to be my friend? I have a good sense of self-esteem and can imagine that there are people who would enjoy my company, but something is fishy with my Facebook account.

A little explanation seems to be in order. When my mother was in the hospital in Arizona, I went there to keep her company and to try to sort out the medical issues. At first there was drama. Her health was touch and go, and there were doctors, nurses, technicians, gnomes, yeti, and who knows what else going in and out of the room. I was absorbed in the crisis, but once that was passed, things changed. Mom slept a lot, and I tried to fill my time sitting around and doing whatever there is to do in hospitals when no bells are going off.

I watched television. I like television, but after a while, I need something else to do. When that time came, I went to the cafeteria and ate. Eating and watching television can often sustain me, but day after day it got old. I had my computer, and I was using it to keep my job updated on what was going on, but I didn't have enough expertise to do much more. That was the context for this deluge of people wanting to be my friend.

In my boredom, I joined Facebook. Sitting at my unconscious mother's bedside, I went to their site, followed the directions, and I was in. I should have become suspicious when I was able to do it so easily. The only times this has happened has been when I was about to be scammed. Why is it that scammers are the only computer entities whose directions I can follow?

Anyway, I got an account, but then what? My wife and daughter are among the millions who can sit on Facebook for hours and be entertained. I go on, see if anyone has found me who I want to have looking for me, and move on. It's pretty boring. As it is, when I turn it on, a guy I knew in college who now lives in Cincinnati is on. He appears with a picture of himself with his right eye grotesquely distorted by some sort of camera trick. His friends from Cincinnati are telling him that they went to a concert or that they want the Reds to beat some other team, but what has this got to do with me?

My wife tells me that I'm doing this wrong, and no doubt this is true. Like a lot of the stuff in the new millennium, the possibilities far exceed my capacity to attend. Facebook could probably make my coffee in the morning or do my taxes, but I'll never know it. Besides, no one has to tell me that I'm missing something essential with this, even though hundreds and hundreds of people are standing ready to do just that.

Which gets me to the point. A few days ago, I scrolled down to the part of Facebook that lists the people who would like to "friend" me. By the way, I hate the way cute new words keep coming out to meet the needs of the technoboobs who we knew were pathetic before they all became billionaires. The one that comes closest to being a sharp No. 4 pencil in my eye is the use of the word *fun* as an adjective. The following sentence is an example of what I mean: "Would it be funner to push a computer geek over a cliff or to drop one into the ocean?"

Anyway, I know that people are attracted to me, at least in the way that they are attracted to ugly dogs at animal shelters, but the list was astronomical. Here was a dammed-up well of people, all of whom were anxiously hoping that I would become their friend. I imagined them in a big auditorium, shooting out of their chairs, waving their hands, and squealing, "Pick me! Pick me!" like third-graders who actually know an answer and want to prove it.

I regally continued to scroll through the list, and as I did, it kept expanding. More and more people were added, sometimes faster than I could scroll. I supposed that the social network was notifying everyone that I was on and looking through the list of possible friends. Everyone who had been waiting for this marvelous opportunity was jumping in. Some of the names were people I recognized. My son and his wife, my daughter, my wife—all of them had requested my friendship. I resolved to call them up and assure them that they had more than my friendship—I love them.

Neighbors who had eaten hot dogs and homemade potato salad around my pool were asking in, as were people with the same last names as some of my friends. I chalked these up to the fact that my friends must have told them about me, and they were hoping that they could be included in the few who were basking in the warmth of my affection. I made a mental note to mention this to these friends, hoping to let them down gently. At my age, there are only so many that I can truly connect with in a deep way. I could be acquaintances to these "second degree of separation" requests, but that is all.

Here's where it began to get fishy. I began to get friend requests from people who had no apparent connection to me at all. At first I thought these were people I knew and was just forgetting. I forget lots of things, people I've met included. I was mildly embarrassed by this and decided to get some ginkgo biloba, but the list grew to the point that I realized that even my mental failings couldn't be the whole reason for these requests. Who were these people? What could they possibly expect of me? I'm only one man. And what is so interesting about me that the starting nose tackle of the New England Patriots would want to be my friend?

I clearly needed expert advice. When the social scene gets blurry, my wife usually steps in and clears things up. I called her over and showed her the list. Now, Marcie is drawn to people the way mass is drawn to black holes. Put her in a line at the automobile registry, and in fifteen minutes she'll be exchanging shopping tips with angry nineteen-year-olds from Detroit and lanky refugees from the Sudan. She identified a few of those requests, like my cousin from Saratoga's next-door neighbor who we met at a traffic light six years earlier, but mostly she told me that the site was selecting people who might have some interest in me. It was kind of like I was being set up for blind dates. Like I was a hobby for the machine, which recognized that I would never be able to connect on my own, and so it was doing it for me.

These days, I stay off Facebook for the most part. I still don't understand it, and I'm beginning to get weirded out by the Cincinnati guy's eye.

TRAVEL
and
OTHER THINGS.

Monkey Shovels

I hate to travel, especially on airplanes. The idea of packing my favorite things and trusting that strangers will bring them to me thousands of miles away seems like insanity. I get very anxious at airport security points. I always have the nagging worry that I've packed a gun in my luggage and forgotten it's there. The fact that I don't own a gun does little to dispel the guilt and fear I feel over this. I figure that if they're checking me, maybe they have a reason. After all, they have uniforms. They have badges. They see people like me all the time, trying to look harmless. Some aren't harmless. What if that's me? I know this is irrational, but fortunately age has taught me that reason isn't that important most of the time.

Anyway, I hate to travel, especially by plane. It's not that I fear flying; I usually feel fine about it. I don't mind meeting people on planes. I like peanuts. I even can sleep on long flights. I just don't like to travel.

This anti-travel feeling is bolstered by my love of home. I like my home. I always have. Even when I shared an unheated four-room slum with three twenty-year-old drunks, a dog, and two cats, I loved my home. Even when the toilet froze, I loved my home. I think it's genetic. My father loved his home, in the way that only Sicilians who have finally gotten a piece of land of their own can love their home.

My grandfather was a Sicilian immigrant who somehow found himself in Connecticut. He bought a falling-down storefront with two frayed apartments in it, and immediately stopped working. Even an Edward Hopper-style dump qualified him as a patrone, and patrones did not work. (Sadly for my grandmother, patrones' wives worked. Their kids worked, too, but not patrones.)

I most definitely love my home now, and I think its borderline crazy to leave it. I have cable television. I have a pool table. I have at least six couches. What's not to love?

My wife is a fabulous woman. Smart, beautiful, hardworking, and everything else anyone could want in a wife, except for one or two little things. Regarding travel and my feelings about it, she's just unreasonable. She can't imagine a trip not worth taking. A hike through the Mato Grasso jungle sounds just ducky. How about the magnificent epic of the caribou migration on the Arctic Circle? Fabulous. Over time, I've been able to let her know that my ideal vacation is for her to take the kids and go anywhere in the world she'd like. I'll stay home and take care of the dogs.

She has often accepted this strategy, but the woman loves me. (Who wouldn't?). She likes my company, even when I'm convulsively clutching my little backpack in the corner of the stateroom on a cruise in the Caribbean or hiding my jewelry in my underwear before venturing out onto the mean streets of Venice. This means that occasionally I have to surrender good sense and travel.

We've developed a few policies that make the ordeal a little closer to palatable for me. Most important among these is that we almost never travel alone. She needs someone who would risk their lives on zip lines with her. She needs someone to eat midnight snack with her in pirate bars that would scare Obi Wan. She needs someone to snap pictures of us together in front of boats and churches and palm trees. I need the safety of numbers. It's the weakest of the herd that the predators pick off. I don't have to outrun everyone, just one of the others, and so escape to drink at the waterhole another day.

Over the last few years, we've traveled with two other couples. They've traveled with each other for decades, including hiking across Southeast Asia, India, and Afghanistan. Just the kind of leisurely vacation someone like me would enjoy. Knowing Marcie's love of travel, they invited us to go with them to Costa Rica. Now, it wouldn't be fair to characterize these people as cruel or insensitive. They were just ignorant of the fact that travel isn't for everyone. If they hadn't broken their decades-long tradition of going places together, it would have saved me from the terrors of international travel.

It was a dream for Marcie. Usually, she has to do all the travel planning, factoring in the truth that I will never have a good time until after we're home and the pictures are printed. The woman is nothing if not an optimist, though, and she eternally believes that my travel phobia is temporary. In this case, our friend Steve made all the arrangements.

Like a dutiful wife, Marcie went online and got a beautiful brochure of our impending trip. There was the villa we were to stay in. Breathtakingly perched on a cliff, overlooking both the Pacific at sunset, and a charming and graceful town; it had four bedrooms, an infinity pool, a full kitchen, with a housekeeper to cook and clean. The brochure continued with the satellite television, mahogany woodwork throughout, and a twenty-four-hour-a-day phone number of Raul, the concierge, who had lived in New Jersey for ten years.

In her good-hearted way, Marcie was seeking to soften the blow of having to spend a week in this pit of despair, and she thought she'd done just that, except for the last item mentioned. This was a caution just in case, you know, not that it would happen, but just something to know if it did come up. The last item said, "Do not fight the monkeys for food."

All my life, I was taught that the world is full of dangers. These dangers were never laid out so clearly before, and I, for one, was grateful for it. Now, I've never liked monkeys. I don't trust them. They don't like people, I'm sure. Not fighting them for food, however, had never occurred to me. Now that it was mentioned, I began to obsess about it. (Obsessions are a kind of hobby of mine.)

What kind of monkeys might I have to fight? Would there be one or two king monkeys who swagger through the neighborhood, picking on the weak and infirm? Marlon Brando types of monkeys on motorcycles, with leather caps and sneers for the townsfolk? Were there flocks of those creepy spider monkeys, who would descend on the unwary, getting on their backs, in their hair, going through their pockets and taking whatever they could before the poor victim could jump in the pool and get them off? Those little guys are stronger than they look, and any one of them would die for the rest.

My obsessions continued with thoughts of how you would fight a monkey if you had to. I already said that I don't have a gun. Knives let the enemy get too close. You can't bring a proper anti-monkey weapon on a plane, so it would have to be something I could get once we landed. I finally settled on what I felt would give me the best chance of surviving a monkey fight, and possibly even earning a measure of respect from them. The final decision was a shovel—a good, stout shovel with the kind of handle that gives good leverage and a firm grip. Whang a couple of them with a shovel, and the rest would keep their distance. By the time that they could think about retaliation, I would be home.

These are the thoughts that comforted me through what turned out to be a wonderful week, once the pictures were printed. For the record, I never saw a monkey. I heard that most were being killed by traffic. I should be sad about that, but it's just not working out that way.

The lesson here? It's a big world, and there are all kinds of people in it. Some are tall, some short, some smart, and some not. Because we need to feel that the world can be safe and predictable, we often decide that there is a correct path, and only those on it are living a sensible life. When someone raises questions about the correctness of our decisions, it unsettles us and tends to make us reject them as crazy. This is another of those tricks we play on ourselves to create the illusion of control.

In fact, there are as many paths as there are people, and the large majority of them are correct. I don't like to travel, despite the fact that most people would envy the chances I've had to do it. I do appreciate my luck, and I know I'm a lucky man. (A *very* lucky man at that.) As of today, I'm using my monkey shovel to prop up my back fence until I can do something to really fix it.

Baggage Claim

For the most part, I like airports. I like the breezy kinds of stores they have, the big windows, the food you can almost eat while holding it in your lap, and the people watching. I like carry-on luggage. The kind with lots of zippers and pockets, where you can pack all the essentials for a siege, just in case. I always go to the airport equipped with plenty of books, layers of comfortable clothes, cough drops, my camera, tissues, batteries, extra glasses, a small flashlight, and any number of clever gadgets that I've accumulated over the years. Come to think of it, it may be the gadgets that I like more than the airport, but I like both.

Over the last couple of decades, my gadgetry has changed. This has been due to politics, technology, and age. When I first started to travel, I always had a Swiss army knife in the front of my small backpack. It was a comfort to know that if a screw came loose or a bottle cap got surly, I was ready. I especially liked the small pliers it had. I never tired of showing it off, although it seldom was able to repair anything. That particular item has gone the route of powdered wigs, of course, since 9/11. For me, the security gained is negated by the security lost. The people around me can be comfortable knowing that they're not in danger of being corkscrewed by me, but if I crack a fingernail, I know that help is far away in my checked baggage.

For the last couple of years, I've brought along my laptop. It presents some inconveniences, such as having to remove it at the security checkpoint, but there are times that I find it a most pleasant diversion. Coupled with my digital camera, I can download (upload?) any pictures I've taken, edit them, and fill my time on the imitation leather seats at the gate. Having a laptop has altered my luggage, though, and I have to admit that I take this kind of change rather poorly.

For many years, I carried a backpack. The backpack I carried changed over time. It started in the sixties with something Army surplus, the rattier the better, progressed through the L.L. Bean years, and continued into the advent of chic, expensive leather, but it was always indisputably a backpack. This means two shoulder straps, at least forty zippers, something Velcro, one of those trendy mountain-climbing clips you see everywhere, and ancillary handles for carrying when necessary. The laptop won't fit properly in one of those. I know, I've tried. Oh sure, they're probably making them bigger now, but I'm too stubborn to go that route, so now it's a briefcase.

It's not that I really mind. The briefcase model does pretty much the same job as the backpack, but it makes a different statement. A backpack says rough and ready. It says free spirit. It reminds me that I used to hitchhike places back in the day. Backpacks carry equipment, guy stuff. Briefcases say city dweller, great at making reservations, but not someone to be relied on to gnaw off a limb to escape being trapped in the wilderness. A briefcase can be a little effete, faintly feminine beside a backpack. I'm sure of my manhood, but I have to work a little harder to do it now that I carry a briefcase.

That's not the only drawback. Lately my wife has been getting briefcases for free at work. I can't resist free. This, of course, forces me to advertise whatever firm or product is on the outside of the case. Now I'm in danger of unwanted human contact from people who assume I have some interest in what the logo represents. "Excuse me, do you work for XYZ Mutual Funds? I have your Impossible Ventures Fund. My broker recommended it to me, just before he went to prison." This forces me to explain that I have no idea what XYZ Mutual Funds are; I just have the briefcase. I have an idea about this, though, that has some interesting possibilities. I'm considering having one made up with a phony company like Acme Medical Waste Storage or EZ-Glow Nuclear Products, and see who has questions about those ventures. I'll bet I get to sit by myself more often.

I suppose I'll just have to get over this briefcase thing. It's just another part of getting older. (That sentence is meant to get me to the next topic.) As I've aged, I've had to make other modifications to my travel patterns. Now I need pills, pills, and more pills. You might already know how I feel about modern medicine, but if you don't, let me give you a quick synopsis. Every time I go for a checkup, I get something new prescribed. Blood pressure, cholesterol, allergies—something prompts my doctor to write me up for another pill.

I don't accept this easily. I refuse any medicines that are just intended to treat minor symptoms. Symptoms are messages from god. It's not a good idea to keep the phone off the hook when these messages are sent. They might only be celestial telemarketing, but you can only tell by hearing the message. Besides, I think that taking a pill to stop one thing only creates another. Despite this, I end up having to carry and keep track of several medications, calling for a compartment in my carry on.

As for over-the-counter stuff, I have to admit that I'm an absolute sucker for nifty packaging. I bring along a few aspirins in those individual foil envelopes, rolls of antacids, little plastic pods with half a dozen Band-Aids and so on, all part of my personal survival kit.

By the way, I know that this is a digression, but who designs Band-Aids these days? I liked it when you got big rectangles, small rectangles, and dots. When you buy a box of them today, you get irregular trapezoids, isosceles triangles, and Rorschachs that must fit somewhere, but never where you have a booboo.

Okay, back to the over-the-counter stuff. It's part of the growing list of things I tote to feed my obsessive nature, but twenty years ago, my backpack was unencumbered by anything even remotely related to health needs. The closest to medicine I got then was a couple of packs of gum and maybe a Slim Jim. It's a little unsettling when your luggage is a testament to your mortality.

I must admit that airports today have substantial differences from when I first started hanging around in them. I remember seeing grandpas and grandmas waiting at terminal gates to greet their families as they came for yearly visits. I remember being able to park just outside of the doorways without concern of being arrested and disappearing into a secret prison in Santo Domingo. Lines were shorter, luggage traveled for free, and you were guaranteed a school cafeteria-quality meal served by a polite woman who didn't have to make change for a fifty when you wanted an extra bag of pretzels.

Despite this perhaps false nostalgia, you can't beat the entertainment of waiting at an airport gate. Recently I watched an unshaven, 240-pound, beer-bellied cowboy anxiously trying to keep his caged Persian kitty happy on its first flight from Reno to Denver. His mustache quivered when the cat cried inside of its brand-new, quilted Vera Bradley feline carrier. He just couldn't listen to that prissy puff ball without responding. He cradled it to his chest, rubbing it and crooning something indescribably simpering. When he noticed that I was staring, he apologized, clearly worried about the cat, saying, "It's her first time on a plane. She's soooo upset." You can't pay for that kind of entertainment.

This last trip, I watched two separate moms with kids on leashes. I hadn't seen that in years. Both kids needed to be leashed too. They were so poorly behaved that I thought of the cowboy's kitty carrier. There must be a market for Kiddie Cages or Brat Barriers. Anyway, the thing I really noticed was that these leashes were both connected to the kids by a soft cloth harness, and the harness was attached to a backpack.

The OK Corral

For no good reason, today I find myself in the Great American West. Actually, that isn't entirely accurate. I have a very good reason to be here, just not a pleasant one. My eighty-six-year-old mother decided that this would be a good place to have a cardiac emergency. She was visiting my cousin and her e-x-t-e-n-d-e-d family, and it hit the fan, so here I am. Over the last week or so, I've learned tons about stuff I didn't know or care existed.

The first thing I did when I arrived was get to the hospital. I've been in hospitals before, but not for more than an hour or two, usually visiting friends and once for a little more time when I had a colonoscopy. The bottom line is that hospitals aren't what they might seem to the uninitiated.

My education began when I told my mother's primary doctor that I intended to sleep in the chair in my mother's room. He told me I was welcome to stay, but that "no one sleeps in a hospital." I thought he was taken aback by my singular devotion to my mom. That wasn't what he meant. He meant that no one sleeps in a hospital. The longest time a patient goes without being poked, timed, squeezed, turned, plugged in (or unplugged), measured, bounced, or dragged is two hours.

Don't make the mistake of thinking that means there is ever a two-hour period of peace. There is always a buzzer, gong, pager, or whistle going off in the room. These were especially disturbing at first, when we thought that they might mean something important. The good nurses usually popped in. Without a word, they'd hit a switch and the alert would stop.

After the first few days, I became curious and asked what one meant. I was told that they would ask the cardiologist, who would consult with the respiratory therapist, who meets with the primary doctor, who is on rounds in the Philippines right now, but he'll be back before the Arctic is completely melted. And if your grandchildren are still alive and interested, he'll tell them why the siren is screaming in your ear.

The next thing I learned is that doctors don't always know everything. My mother was fortunate enough to have one of the doctors who knew that. The lesson was taught kind of by accident, when our 108-pound, eleven-and-a-half-year-old primary physician had a run-in with the 280-pound cardiologist.

I know I'm digressing here, but I have to say that it's disconcerting to have a woman of this size come sweating into your hospital room, lean against the wall to catch her breath, and then wheeze instructions on heart health. "We (huff puff) think (huff puff) your mom (wheeze), has had a (eyes roll up in her head, she staggers for a second, regains equilibrium) stroke."

The primary says "Golly, do ya think so? Because I don't. I think she's got an infection, and maybe a stroke, and maybe not. But maybe. I asked my best friend Uncle Bobby. He's a doctor, too, you know, and he doesn't think it was a stroke."

Uncle Bobby is a neurologist and has been since Truman was president. I'm told this is good, because my mother has a new pacemaker and can't have an MRI. Uncle Bobby doesn't need them. In fact, he doesn't believe in them. He reminds me of one of the doctors who recommended Camel cigarettes in the magazine ads. "Well (phew), I did an (huff) exam and I (gasp) saw clots."

"Clots! Zowie, that's bad isn't it? Clots! If you see any again, will you let me look? I'll be good, I promise."

These are the conversations we aren't meant to hear. What did work out was that everyone agreed that we needed to focus on what to do to make my mom feel better, and since all the doctors easily agreed on what that would be, we moved forward.

I have no doubt that these things are true in any hospital, but there's something about the West that we New Englanders don't get. People here are nice. We're not used to that. Nice makes us nervous.

Cars stop to let us cross the street. What's with that? If cars stop like that at home, it usually means the driver is trying to get off a better shot.

People here think they have the best climate anywhere. The weatherman must be unbelievably bored. All anyone really needs is a thermometer. Will it be over 110 today or not? I've yet to meet anyone who lives here who hasn't asked me about the weather back home. The lady at the cafeteria counter said, "Where ya from, hon?" When I told her Boston, she got an odd grin and said, "What's the temperature like back there?"

"Seventy-seven," I said.

She got a smug look and said, "Humid, I'll bet." Humidity seems to be the antichrist here. Humid, she says, though it's a hundred and seven out right now. Perfect weather if you have scales or thorns.

I was lucky with my timing, though. I got here just in time for snake season. The local paper had that as a headline this morning. It seems that it has something to do with hibernation and temperatures. I was interested to learn that the Phoenix/Scottsdale area has twelve different varieties of rattler. You don't have to know which one bites you; the hospitals are ready to treat any of them. You have to be thankful for that.

Another lucky thing for a New Englander is that the hospital where I'm spending my days is a "weapons free" campus. Westerners have a different sensibility about weapons in general and firearms in particular. In Boston, you can be fairly certain that you aren't the only person in a public place that isn't packing. Here, if someone finds out you don't have a gun, they politely get you one and promise not to let anyone else know of your shame.

Anyway, locals tell me I don't have to worry about snakes, as long as I stay on the sidewalk. I'm taking their word for it, but I must admit, I don't understand how the snakes feel about this arrangement.

Shameless Exhibitionism

I had an idea for a new vacation resort. I got it several years ago, when my wife arranged for us to go to a Club Med. It was of course located on a magnificent island, and even more of course, it was staffed by some of the world's most beautiful people. It seemed like every one of them was getting ready for an Olympic tryout or had just signed with a professional soccer team in Brazil. These people were unwaveringly cheerful and went out of their way to invite everyone for beach volleyball, windsurfing, or a quick cliff dive. In fact, they went more than out of their way to invite us; they were flat persistent in trying to get everyone involved in some vigorous activity or other.

For a while, I assumed that this persistence was part of their job. Given that most of the guests were Americans and seemed prone to sedentary pursuits, I thought that they had to work hard to see to it that we guests had a good time. I figured that these Australian, Italian, French, and Dutch eye candies were being coerced into seeing to it that all guests were smiling at all times. I pictured a snarling, hairy-forearmed Saddam type in some hidden office, driving the staff to greater heights of exertion in order to save some kidnapped family member in a dank cellar somewhere.

The truth came to me in a moment of realization. These people weren't desperate to see to it that I enjoyed myself; they were mocking my well-earned pot belly and provoking my few remaining shallow breaths. It was all so clear! It was just like high school reunions. People don't go to them for the limp salad and reheated macaroni. The only people who willingly attend those affairs are those who lost weight or got rich. They're there to show off. The same was true at Club Med.

I know when I'm being laughed at. I began right then and there to develop an idea for a vacation spot of my own. I'd call it Club Fred. The staff at Club Fred would all have to be morbidly obese. They would have to chain smoke and breathe heavily just from getting off a couch. No Olympic athletes here, unless they were on the Competitive Eating Team. No one working at Club Fred could ever have been a cheerleader or on any sports team. They would be required to trip over something at least once an hour. Just thinking about it made me want to start getting investors together. Why go to a fat farm when you could be the slimmest person at a beautiful resort just as you are right now?

Anyway, the idea was immediately quashed by my lovely but fit wife, who chewed me out for being negative, and by the way, how about scuba lessons from gorgeous Jean Claude? Yeah, right. I let it go, filed away with all the other humiliations I've accumulated because of my athletic shortcomings, but it reemerged recently.

The whole concept returned full blown during the Boston Marathon. The marathon is a big event in our area and even bigger to my family. My wife ran it once upon a time, so it's become a ritual to go and sit beside the road and cheer the runners as they pass. There are helicopters flying overhead, trucks filled with reporters from the local television stations, state police motorcycles, balloon vendors, ice cream vendors, and probably a million onlookers as skinny people from all over the world pass in clusters and clots, pouring water on their heads and receiving encouragement from strangers and friends throughout the twenty-six miles. I've never watched it without feeling miserable.

There are tens of thousands of ordinary people who have trained themselves to be able to do this extraordinary thing. They run countless miles in countless hours to come to Boston on one particular day and make people like me feel rotten about ourselves. Don't be mistaken by their claims that they just want to feel their own sense of achievement. They are in it for the same reasons as the Club Med sociopaths. They enjoy running by the flabby millions and gloating.

I know this for a fact. And once I realized it, I began to express my bitterness. I began to whisper to the stragglers. I began to tell them that they should just quit. They weren't going to win. Some Kenyan had gone by an hour ago. They were just torturing themselves. Why not stop right here and have a Coke and some cupcakes? It was an amazingly uplifting feeling until my wife overheard me and sent me home.

Anyway, I have an idea about these egotistical marathoners too. If all they want is to feel their own inner achievements, then why don't they run the thing at night? Why not pick some random night, get one of those lamps that coal miners wear, and run the thing from midnight until four or five in the morning? Run it with no one watching who could feel bad. They could still get the sense of having done something monumental, and I wouldn't have to know about it.

Actually, as I get older, I get other ideas about this whole exhibitionist thing. I've begun to make stuff up about myself, so that they can get a taste of their own medicine. I told a svelte MD cousin-in-law that I didn't swim because of the trauma of my years as a Navy Seal. I signed the parents' directory at my daughter's school as Colonel Vincent D'Aleo (ret.). I'm sure I'll think of other things to protect myself against the onslaught of self-promoters as the need arises.

Nine-Tenths of the Law

Everyone I know has their own Chinese restaurant. It wasn't always that way. When I was a kid, my family didn't have one. It didn't matter too much, because no one I knew had one. It wasn't because we were too poor or lived in a bad neighborhood. It was more because in the place and time in which I grew up, Chinese restaurants were pretty scarce. Anyway, I have one now, and so do all the people I know. To be clear, we don't each exclusively have one, but we have them just the same. I not only have my own Chinese restaurant, I have my own Costco too. In fact, I've had several of each, but never two at the same time.

It's a peculiar process, getting your own Chinese restaurant and Costco. It actually involves a series of delicate maneuvers that can be so subtle that it's hard to know that it's happening. My first came in the sixties, when I was in college. My friends and I discovered an apparently orphaned Chinese spot near Cleveland Circle in the Brighton section of Boston. It was in the middle of a block, waiting despondently to be adopted by someone.

It was actually its misfortune to be found by my friends and me. We were too young and irresponsible to care for a place. It was called the New Far East restaurant, but we renamed it the New Far Out, in keeping with the vernacular of the times. I vaguely remember that the staff greeted us sadly and apprehensively each time we showed up, which was typically late at night after conscientious weekends of highly focused study. (At least that's what our parents would have liked to think.) I can't remember ordering anything that wasn't fried and cheap. It was the only Chinese place I've ever gone to that served bread.

Anyway, we were lousy tippers, too loud, too ignorant of the subtleties of Asian cuisine to be the ideal adoptive owners. The best I can say is that we never skipped out on a check, though some of our friends did. My first inkling that I had emotionally connected with the New Far Out was the sense of disapproval I had upon hearing that others had not payed the bill. It was a curious feeling, surprising at that time because it was the era of "sticking it to the man." I had little moral conflict about skipping out on the Polynesian Temple or the Jade Palace, but not the New Far Out; it was ours. It was one of those occasional moments when you realize that something is different than it was before, something primal and internal. I had my first Chinese restaurant.

It was an age of innocence, but a necessary one. My relationship with the New Far Out couldn't last, but it was sweet while it was there.

I'm not the most worldly of diners, but I've been around a little since then. I've had a number of rewarding relationships with Szechuan delights and Cantonese tidbits, including a long-term committed one with an eatery called The Wok that still holds a special place in my heart and to which I still sometimes go out of my way for Udon Noodle Soup lunch. But my relationship with The Wok is like the one between the Robert Mitchum gunslinger and the Rhonda Fleming cagy, old saloon girl. There's a deep understanding and comfort, but the thrill is gone.

My Chinese restaurant now is a local joint in a strip mall, called the Blue Orchid. It sits between a drop-in veterinarian and a barber shop. It's not really much better or different from a million other places just like it. The General Gao's Chicken and Hot and Sour Soup taste the way I think they should, because I'm used to the way they make them there.

The waitresses come and go, staying for a year or two and disappearing. I know this is my place, because I'm there to greet the new servers, to break them in, and to teach them what I like and how I like it. They can be said to have completed their training when they bring my wife her iced tea as we're being seated or when they act surprised when I ask to have my shumai fried instead of steamed.

Getting your own Costco is kind of the same. I know that all Costcos have the same stuff in them, but that doesn't matter. My wife and I go to Costco nearly every week. We usually go on Saturday morning, enjoy the "buffet" of samples, buy lots of stuff we didn't know we needed until we saw it, get a dollar-fifty hot dog, and leave. It's an integral part of our marriage.

The only odd thing about it is that it just can't happen in someone else's Costco. Someone else's Costco seems much more like a warehouse, and not a nice warehouse. Someone else's Costco is filled with dark corners, and the dog food and AAA batteries are in the wrong places. The people who work there look at you funny if you take more than one sample of cheesecake, and the other shoppers know you're a stranger and keep a hard eye on you.

I've tried to overcome this feeling, to gut it out, but I haven't been able to get over my own foreignness in someone else's Costco. I can't get past the feeling that I'm surrounded by aliens who look normal, but about whom there is something essential that's just wrong. Somewhere in the background there should be spooky music playing. I'm pretty sure that strangers in my Costco feel the same way that I do about it. It's no one's fault, but something changes inside you when you get your own Costco.

These things might hold true for other places. I haven't thought it completely through. I'm sure it holds for pizza places, but that seems too obvious to mention. It doesn't hold for Staples, and I think someone should let them know about it. I can't get close to a Staples the way that I can get close to a Chinese restaurant or a Costco. Intellectually, I know that a Staples should be able to have a soul in that same way that other places can, but I just don't feel it. It's as if there's a kind of Staples attachment disorder. I admit that it might be me, and I have to say that I haven't been to all the Staples possible, but so far, they're all orphans.

Snow Days

Teaching school can be a little like not growing up. The vacations are terrific, the hours aren't bad, and most days are at least a little bit interesting. It isn't a career that I considered before I found myself fifteen years into it, but now I'm grateful that I've been able to do it. It happens that today is the beginning of my summer vacation, a perfect day to wax nostalgic.

One of the best things about working at a school is getting snow days. I get giddy listening to weather reports on wintry nights, trying to anticipate a five a.m. call giving me the day off. There's always a second's hesitation while I weigh the values of a free day tomorrow against a makeup day tacked on to the end of the calendar, but it's the pull of immediate gratification that most often wins out. Once in a while, snow days can be a surprise. The furnace at school went out one morning, so we were off until it was fixed, or another time the basement flooded and we stayed home until that was cleaned up. There is nothing wrong with an unexpected call in the morning. The sheets feel especially good on mornings when you know you can crawl back under for another two hours.

Even in the years when there have been no snow days, teaching has been a pretty good gig. It's been changing, though, in the years since I started. I don't know if it's just me, but it seems like there is a greater emphasis on teaching facts and information now. I suppose that it comes from feeling the need to compete with other countries whose students seem to have learned more of them than ours have. There is also a desire to measure the teaching and learning that takes place in schools. Measuring is best done with clear, concrete scales, and the teaching of a quantity of information is more easily measured than the quality of what is learned.

My own personal tendency in the classroom is neutrality toward the teaching and learning of facts, unless the facts are connected to bigger ideas or concepts. It always seems that there are some kids who are predisposed to gather and retain bushels of facts about the history of the armored car or horses or the battles of the Civil War. They very likely learned them because they were interested in these things. It always seems like these kids grow up to be engineers or professors or to work online in their mother's spare room. It would take a motivated student and a persistent teacher an awfully long time to master all they know if it weren't important to them. I sometimes wonder if it wouldn't be better to use this time and energy in other ways.

It's true that different people learn differently. Some of us are more comfortable getting bit by factual bit of a story until a pattern takes shape and we understand it. Others get crazy with the bit-by-bit approach. They want to know what the idea is before they get the facts. Once they know it, they can fill in the details that got them there.

Actually, all of us have some of each of these kinds of properties in us, but each of us has them in different degrees. The danger, I think, lies in the extremes. Mountains of facts don't have to integrate into patterns; they can remain just disconnected pieces of information. And lots of big ideas don't have to result in anything specific happening either.

As I said earlier, I'm neutral about teaching facts, unless they're connected to bigger ideas. I try to present both. I try to select facts that refer to the major tides of history. For instance, geography is good when you use it to explain why Poland has been invaded so often or how Venice got so rich. I also choose facts that have good emotional impact. Those are remembered, and they tend to invite further study into a subject. Before I teach the great explorations of the fifteenth and sixteenth centuries, I make it a point to be sure my middle school boys learn how sailors went to the bathroom on ships like Magellan's. It won't turn up on a standardized test or help them with a career path, but they're more attentive to the other information if you slip in something like that once in a while.

I sometimes think I do my best teaching when I'm digressing. I learned when my son Michael was small that kids aren't always taking in the things we think they are. While showing him how to tie his shoes, I used a very scientific "backward chaining" technique I'd learned from my behavioral psychologist sister-in-law. She taught me that when presenting a specific sequence of steps, starting from the last step and working backward is more effective than starting from the beginning and risking frustration when the kid stops at every failure. This strategy not only made sense, but it allowed me to do it in a different way than the other dads. In other words, it had a snob appeal that I can't resist.

I started with that little double tug you give the bows when you're finished, at least that's what I meant to start with, but Michael, serious student that he always was, began by straightening his cuffs, mimicking the motion I did just after the tug. I'm a creature of habit, and I unconsciously do that every time I tie my shoes. To kids, your digressions can be just as meaningful as the intended direction of your words.

Yet there are things that must just be memorized. Reading and math are full of important pieces of information, and your life will be diminished if you don't know them. For some, physics and Latin declensions are important and vibrant subjects, with facts that will sustain them financially and emotionally. For the rest of us, can't we learn the big ideas behind these subjects? Memorize a smattering of facts that will allow us to understand the basics and then move on?

At one point, there was an attempt to integrate subjects by connecting learning about algebra or geometry, for instance, to problems and situations that might have some interest to kids. It seemed like a good idea to me. Maybe that's because that's how I learn, but I'm willing to bet that most kids introduced to this kind of learning do better. I'm not sure if this is true, but I heard once that although our students couldn't match those in other countries for how much they'd learned, they far outdid their competition when it came to things like Nobel Prizes for theoretical subjects.

Indian Head Pennies

Today, through a convergence of circumstance, I walked down the street to the barbershop. Allow me to claim credit for avoiding at least five digressions to describe those circumstances.

On the way, I found five pennies and a dime, and one of the pennies was a wheat penny, 100 percent copper. I found this bounty at random intervals along the side of the fairly main road on which I live. What that suggests to me is that they aren't the tragic result of a pocket hole or a mistake made by the driver of an armored car. A bunch of people must have cared so little about their change that they tossed it out rather than carry it. Remember, there is even a wheat penny in this jettisoned treasure.

If you're old enough, you remember when all pennies were wheat pennies. If you're my age, you even remember when, every once in a while, you found an Indian Head penny in your change. I was actually luckier than most in this regard, although at the time it didn't feel that way. My family's grocery store was named D'Aleo and Sons, and as one of the Sons, I was expected to contribute labor. I had a variety of jobs that I completed with the most sloth and reluctance possible. These included sorting deposit bottles (no convenient can crusher that dispensed receipts, but honest-to-god glass bottles that were picked up by the soda delivery men), stocking shelves, removing snow from the sidewalk, bagging, and as I got old enough, running the cash register.

In retrospect, I don't imagine I was more lukewarm about the quality of my work than any other eleven-year-old, but at the time, all I could think about was getting done and getting out. My father was notoriously grouchy; most of the jobs were monumentally boring, and the rewards were few and far between.

Among these rewards was unlimited access to all snack foods, a perk I fully exploited. My fingers were perpetually greasy from nickel bags of potato chips. I became expert in all facets of candy bars, from the standard male and female Hershey's to the exotic and salty peanut-coated logs that seemed to sit on the counter for months without being purchased. I trained myself to be able to down an entire sixteen-ounce Bubble-Up without stopping, a feat that I hoped would pay off sometime when a girl was watching.

Another, more relevant benefit was access to the change drawer. It happened that there were many down periods when manning the register was necessary, but when customers were scarce. During those moments, I was allowed to sift through the change in the drawer to enhance my coin collection. Of course, I was required to replace any money I took, but I was able to become the only boy in my circle who had a complete penny book, 1941 to 1963. I had all three steel 1943s. I even had the legendary 1909s-VDB. VDB stands for Victor D. Brenner, the man who designed the coin that replaced the Indian Head penny.

One day, while going through the coins, I found five Indian Heads. Every once in a while, one would show up, but five was unheard of. I imagined that some kid's urge for a Milky Way outweighed his prudent speculation for his financial future, and he liquidated his coin collection. In the classic economic paradigm, his foolishness became my good luck.

So what has happened that I can now walk to the barbershop and find a wheat penny by the side of the road (not to mention the other fourteen cents)? The answer is obvious: inflation-induced insanity. I pick up pennies because I remember when they were worth something in themselves; and dimes, dimes were a bonanza. The fifteen cents I rescued today would have purchased a large buttered popcorn at the Strand Theatre's Saturday double feature, and buttered popcorn in those days was actually popped in front of you, and—yes, I'm going to say it—was doused with actual butter. That constitutes a real benefit. What is non-dairy topping, anyway? Seems like a pretty wide loop to cast over something we're meant to eat.

Today, fifteen cents buys, what? What can you get for fifteen cents? Here are a couple of ideas.

1. Probably a fistful of those white plastic sleeves that hold the pop-up buttons for turkeys that tell you when they're done
2. A large, healthy night crawler from the automatic bait dispenser I saw once in front of a tackle shop that has since closed
3. A copy, made at the old library in my town (We're building a new one, so copies will probably be a quarter now, but I'm sure the machine will accept credit and debit cards.)
4. Eh...umm...err... Well, you get the idea.

What's to be done? I can't condone throwing away money. It goes against my compulsive nature and sets a terrible precedent. It's disrespectful to those others in the world who have to go without and who would find a real use for fifteen cents.

For myself, I've found a system. I start with pennies. If I have five or less, I keep them in my pocket and use them to "even out" bills when I shop. As an example, if I buy a donut for seventy-six cents, I use one of the pennies to get the bill back to seventy-five. I then get a quarter, instead of two dimes and four pennies. Any change I get that's not a penny, I put in a jar beside my bed. (It's a nice jar, made by a potter who had a yard sale, and it looks good on my nightstand.)

If I have more than five pennies, I put the excess in stacks of five on the mantle in my room. As my "pocket pennies" are diminished, I replace them from the mantle. Eventually, the jar fills up, and I roll the change into paper sleeves and take it to the bank. From past experience I can tell you that the jar holds about ninety dollars. Ninety dollars is an amount I have yet to find as I walk down the street, although I'm hoping.

Now, my system is probably not for everyone. In fact, my wife got jumpy and a little sad when I explained why there were stacks of pennies on the mantle. But there has to be a better way than throwing them out. Maybe just a dish in the kitchen for pennies until you have enough for a pound of butter.

Stacking Toast

It's really easy to get diagnosed today. Every time you turn around, someone is coming up with a new and better way to name whatever you are, do, and/or feel. It's not even necessary to ask for this; it's there whether you're interested or not. Part of it is because we have a natural urge to feel in control of our environment, to feel as though the world is predictable and a little bit safe. The Bible pretty much covers this, when it tells Adam that he has dominion over the animals. If I remember correctly—and I admit that this is a fifty-fifty proposition on a good day—he was supposed to name them. Naming implies control. I assume that trying to know what's going on is deeply inherent to human nature, but I don't think that's the whole story.

These days, there's big money in diagnoses, but when I was younger, it was different. At that time, you didn't get it unless you asked, and then you had to ask a doctor. We lived in ignorance of the exotic dangers and tragic disabilities we were facing, wallowing in the false security of accepting a little misery. What I mean is that back in the day, when we felt sick, sometimes we called the doctor. When we did that, mostly we found out that we had (a) the flu, (b) a cold, (c) a broken arm, and that if we waited a few days, took aspirin and drank clear fluids, we'd either get better or die. If that seems harsh, remember that we only went to the doctor sometimes. More often, when we felt sick, it got explained without resorting to paid experts.

"Dad, my leg hurts."

"Your leg hurts? Your leg hurts? Look at my leg. [At this point, dad would pull up his pant leg and show you a pale, meaty calf.] My leg has hurt since 1935, when my brother hit me with a snow shovel, and you don't hear me complaining."

If this inspirational demonstration didn't suffice, you could tell your mother.

"Mom, my leg hurts."

"Your leg hurts. Your leg hurts. Loraine told me Tuesday that her leg hurts. She has varicose veins that actually look like blue worms. It was pretty interesting. Do you have varicose veins?"

Here, if she hadn't become engrossed in watching bread dough rise, she might ask to see your leg, and if it didn't have blue worms, that was that. You were told to wait a few days and it would get better. Probably. Miraculously, we mostly did get better in a few days. I may be paying for this now, with achy knees and all, but I have had fifty or so years of relative comfort.

The same pattern was clear in school. We didn't have learning disabilities, executive functioning issues, autistic spectrums, gifted-and-talentedness, or advanced placement. Some kids were goofy, a few were bad, a couple of boys knew everything there was to know about dinosaurs, and maybe two of us could hit a hardball out of the lot beside St. Joseph's School. Until we noticed the differences between boys and girls, that was about it for categories.

As you know, things have changed. No one is normal today. We're all special, and I don't necessarily mean that in a good way. I swear that there are people, smart people, who do nothing but think of ways in which we are uniquely in need of help. Coincidentally, they also stand ready to provide the help they show us we need. Okay, I'm guilty of cynicism, but I'm only human.

It peaked for me with RLS. I couldn't believe my ears! RLS, Restless Leg Syndrome. Now, before I go any further, I sincerely hope that I'm not offending anyone who truly suffers from this, but for my whole life I've bounced my legs, squirmed in bed, and shuffled my feet. Until I heard my diagnosis, I never even thought about it. It has gone on for so long and been so constant that it was like the ringing in my ears or the color of my bedroom wallpaper.

Of course it's there, but I forget about it until it's pointed out. It drove my mother crazy, as it did my first wife and every other woman who's spent more than two hours with me. The affliction of RLS pales in comparison with the bruises on my ankles from the repeated kicks I've gotten under tables in restaurants, in movie theaters, and in bed. Be clear, I blame no one for this. I get crazed when I'm with someone who bounces their leg. Maybe it's because they're in a different rhythm than I am, but it's undeniably annoying.

The key is that today we're told not to live with annoying. If we take a pill, annoying isn't necessary, and if we don't take one, annoying can become dangerous and ultimately result in death. Forgive my fatalism, but no matter what, something is going to result in death. I'm not saying to accept real disease passively and suffering if it can be changed, but let's get over the incessant tweaking we're told to endure.

Anyway, the subject is diagnoses, and it's time to get on with it. I'm weird. There it is. I know it. If you didn't know it before, now you do. I'm not sure if weird was a category when I was a kid, but I'm fairly sure that it would have been understandable. It isn't the kind of weird that stands out. You probably wouldn't be scared to wait for a bus beside me or anything. I look pretty normal, but so do most of us. It has taken some time to pinpoint the diagnosis, but it's been done. My wife has finally zeroed in on my main strangeness. I have OCD.

Obsessive Compulsive Disorder is a terrible curse. It debilitates competent and worthy people. It demands more and more time to perform the most cursory tasks. It absorbs lives in elaborate rituals and patterns that even the sufferers see as unnecessary, but they can't stop them. It's one of those afflictions that doesn't present to the naked eye. There is no bleeding or protruding bones, so people with it are often misunderstood and suffer from social stigma as well as the OCD. If I joke about it, I know that for some it's no joke. I mean no disrespect to the real sufferers.

It probably shouldn't be so hard to understand, because it's one of those dysfunctions that are more a matter of degree than being something alien. It's kind of on a spectrum. Most of us have some things we do the same way at the same times, little compulsions or obsessions that go unnoticed, and that's the point. I have little weirdnesses, little quirks that almost no one notices. Almost no one excludes my wife.

It came up on a Sunday morning. Every Sunday morning, we go out to breakfast. We go to the same place, where the waitresses know how I take my coffee. It's a comfortable feeling, and at my age, comfort trumps adventure nine out of ten times. Anyway, Sunday breakfast, I order eggs. Well, I order eggs, home fries, toast, and sausages, but the eggs and toast are the keys to the whole thing. I like eggs with yolks, and I try to watch the fat, so poached is my preferred style.

I like eggs with yolks, and I like to get *all* the yolk. A plate with significant yolk stains leaves me with a feeling of regret. My plates are consistently clean with reference to yolks, but it doesn't happen that way by accident. I do it by stacking my toast. Toast almost always comes sliced in half, a civilized little extra. I wouldn't think of asking for it any other way. That would be silly, and besides, it's unnecessary. I have a method that meets my needs without involving others. I stack my toast.

It's easy, and even a little bit fun. I match the cut pieces of one slice, and then do the same with the other. Once the pieces are matched this way, I place one piece on top of the other, with the sliced lines at perpendiculars. This done, I put my eggs on the top, and eat away. Any yolk oozes nicely into the toast, and with the lines perpendicular, the bottom piece acts as a kind of insurance against lost yolk. It takes more effort and time to describe this process than it does to do it.

I don't ask others to participate in this method, although it wouldn't be a bad idea. I serenely set it up and go about the business of eating breakfast. With this in mind, you can probably imagine my surprise when I looked across the table and saw my wife staring at me. Her expression was hard to describe. There was a little shock, a touch of embarrassment, and a modicum of frustration. Why? I was minding my own business. When she was able to speak again, it wasn't pretty.

"Are you really *that* nuts?"

I refused to respond in kind, even though there was yolk running all over her plate.

"What do you mean?"

"Did I just see you do that with your toast? Did you just do that?"

"Well, this way I get all the yolk." As I spoke, I gazed pointedly at her excessively messy plate.

"You have OCD. You are beyond weird. I married someone with OCD."

Things kind of went downhill for a while after that; breakfast was finished in silence, and the ride home was also quiet. Since then, I think we've achieved a new comfortable equilibrium. We don't speak about it anymore. I certainly don't blame her for being the victim of our need to find names for things we don't readily understand. Back when I was a kid, I would have been commended for being frugal and exercising prudence. Today I have a disorder.

Truth be told, I know I'm a little eccentric about some things, but who cares. I stack my toast still; I did it this morning. I suspect that my wife wished it were different. I don't think she wishes it enough to insist on a medication evaluation, but only time will tell.

The Louisiana Purchase

Lately I've been thinking about the Louisiana Purchase. In case you don't remember, allow me to give a history lesson. Then I'll apply it to life.

It happened around 1800, when Jefferson had a problem. It was just a decade or so after the republic was established, and we had a fair amount going for us as new Americans (not so much if you were an "old American," like the Cherokee, Sioux, Apache, and so on). Jefferson was all for leaving well enough alone. He envisioned a nation of independent yeoman farmers or small-business owners, prosperous and trouble-free.

Unfortunately, Jefferson was having issues with nasty "foreign entanglements" focused primarily on France and the Port of New Orleans. We had the Mississippi River, all fat and lazy, just waiting to be used to carry our stuff to the Gulf of Mexico and the world. It was that pesky Florida panhandle that was the problem. It stretched further into what was Texas and Spain than it does now. New Orleans was part of it, and France controlled it. I don't remember why, but they threatened to close it off to our use, and of course those independent farmers and tradesmen went blooey. They started screaming for war, and Jefferson was stuck trying to sort it out.

On the other side, a different genius was having troubles of his own. Napoleon was in charge of France, and France was having problems. They were saddled with debt from wars, and they weren't in a position to get involved in another one. Napoleon knew that he'd messed with the business of America, and that was messing indeed. It would have been okay if his ideas for foreign colonies were panning out, but no such luck. He wanted to get things cooking for himself in this New World, but Toussaint L'Ouverture had other ideas. He led a slave revolt in Haiti, the Caribbean island Napoleon was counting on to set a good example, and was generally making colonies look like a bad idea. This trio of troublesome tribulations led to a bonanza to the early republic.

You may already know what happened. Jefferson offered to buy New Orleans. Napoleon made a counteroffer. He offered to sell us Louisiana, the entire French holdings on the American continent. Now, this isn't the 2011 Louisiana with the Bayous and Cajuns, but rather the 1800 Louisiana, which stretched to the Canadian border. He wanted fifteen million, which was back when a million dollars was a lot of money. This was before the birth of the television game show, so you had to work hard for a million.

Anyway, Jefferson could see that this really only equaled about three cents an acre, not so bad when you think about it that way. He wanted to go for the deal, but he had the dilemma of not actually having the right to spend that much of the country's money. Napoleon had probably made it clear that this was a limited-time offer, increasing his counterpart's pressure. Jefferson, lover of the Constitution and its guarantee that no government would be bigger than his ideal individual citizen, now had to either usurp power from the people or miss out on the deal of the century (literally).

Of course we know that he went for the deal. We could see that as a testament to his flexibility in the interest of his country or as an example of the basic power of human greed. Either way, it really doesn't factor very much into my recent thinking about the Louisiana Purchase.

More to the point, I love a bargain. Yard sales draw me like a magnet. I think flea markets ought to be mandatory in every town in the country. I often buy stuff I don't need, just because it's cheap. It's probably genetic for me: my father was the same way. To him, the next best thing to getting a bargain was being able to tell everyone exactly how little he paid for something. "I bought that handsaw for a quarter! At the lumberyard, they're selling new ones for eleven dollars, and these old ones are made of much better steel." This would be fleetingly good news if he didn't already have thirty other ones in his basement that were also cheap, but that wasn't the point. The man would have bought typhus if it were cheap.

This is the quality that first attracted me to the Louisiana Purchase. What a deal! If I were Jefferson, I'd have called up all the other countries and let them know.

"Hi, England? It's me, Tom Jefferson. What's new? We haven't talked in a while."

"We're fine over here, thanks. We're in the middle of a little business with Tecumseh and the Indians, but otherwise we're good. As a matter of fact, I just got a sweet deal on five hundred million acres of continent last week."

"Yeah, the Bonapartes were having a moving sale. I just lucked out."

"Yeah, fifteen million. I had to jump fast, you know. The missus was burned at first, because I didn't have time to consult with her. You know how they get, but she's onboard now."

"I was thinking maybe you want to stop over in a while, after we figure out just what we bought, ha ha. We could have a barbecue or something. The wives could talk while we shoot a few buffalo."

I'm pretty sure that's not really how it went, but the immensity of the deal is to be pondered. In one fell financial swoop, we just about doubled in size. How do you imagine Jefferson felt when he first knew he had the chance to buy the whole thing? That kind of choice isn't even once in a lifetime.

So what's to be learned from this? Perhaps it's that hope springs eternal. Jefferson went from being in a mess to being in a position to make history. I'm guessing that he was somewhat out of his league with this part of the presidency. That's not to say that he was unintelligent or insufficiently public spirited. He was the best man for a hundred vital jobs to start the country, but I don't picture him liking the sustained attention and conflict of being the president. I'm probably wrong, but I see him more comfortable with books and his Virginia friends, sitting around the ole plantation, drinking fine wine and talking about the weather.

I can't help but think that the messiness of the problem of New Orleans must have upset him. It's all humid and hazy there, and he was a most meticulous man. From the rim of disaster to one of the greatest real-estate deals of all time has to have some of the fascination I feel. It's like hitting one of those hundred-million-dollar lotteries.

As a rational man, I know the odds for doing something like this are outrageously slim. They're forever telling you things like you'd have an equal chance to be hit by lightning two dozen times while wearing a Panama hat on a Tuesday of an odd-numbered month in the company of a Buddhist monk, a rabbi, and a Catholic priest. I know I'd be better off throwing a dollar bill into my garbage disposal and getting it over with, but still, when it gets up to that hundred million mark, I get to thinking. *Someone* has to win it. One of the tickets that's being sold will be the winner. Why not me? Not only that, but if you don't buy one, you don't get the satisfaction of thinking that you saved a buck; no, you then think that you *could* have won, but you didn't give yourself the chance. There's no getting around it.

Could be that the takeaway from the Louisiana Purchase—besides the obvious river, mountain, lake, prairie, valley, and other views the realtors could sell—is that you put your dollar in and took the ride. But that doesn't quite satisfy on its own either. That kind of thinking also applies to stuff like you should have skipped dessert or you should have worn clean socks. This just ignores the gravity of the situation. You could think of it as evidence of the burgeoning power of our nation. But just a couple of years later, England was taking our sailors off our own ships at sea. If we were so impressive, that wouldn't have been happening.

I keep going back to the serendipity of it all. A while back, there was a "harmonic convergence" of planets, stars, and whatnot, all lining in a way that only happens in a jillion centuries. I imagine the purchase was kind of like that. I just have to stand back in wonder and think about the alignment of circumstances and the colossal stakes involved. Of course there are points of view, matters of opinion, issues of perspective, but all that aside, I like thinking about the sheer good luck that can happen now and then. Jefferson and the rest of the nation fell into a pool of sharks and came out wearing sharkskin suits. It reminds me of the potential for redemption, even in the face of lousy odds. Thanks, Louisiana Purchase.

Tofu

Why is tofu so popular? I know it's good for you, but that can't be the reason. If tofu was your girlfriend, you'd fight with it. It doesn't stand anywhere.

"What do you want to do tonight?"

"I don't care."

"Do you want to get something to eat?"

"I don't care."

Is there anything more infuriating than someone who has no opinions?

Add to that, if you make a decision, neutrality doesn't mean that it will turn out okay. Once again, your girlfriend offers no opinions, but she reserves the right to complain about the decisions you're then forced to make. "I hate spaghetti."

"Why didn't you say so when I suggested we go to the Spaghetti Shack?"

"Well, I didn't know we were going to have spaghetti."

"We went to the Spaghetti Shack. What did you think we would have?"

"Well, I didn't know I couldn't have Chinese food there."

"Did you want Chinese food?"

"Well, I didn't care about it."

You see how this is going. Tofu is like that. It has no taste of its own. It can't even decide on a texture. It could be soft or firm. What else is left? People say that tofu takes on the flavor of the stuff you put it with. Why bother? Why not just eat the stuff you have, and skip the tofu?

For a while, tofu was trendy. Thirty years ago, you were kind of cool if you knew about it. That is, you were kind of cool if you weren't one of the billions of Asians who ate it almost daily. It isn't their fault that they did this; they might have been forced to. Tofu is also a good source of protein, and if you have more soybeans than you can use (and who doesn't have more of them than they can use?), making tofu is understandable. Anyway, for about four days thirty years ago, tofu was kind of trendy, but once you got through that period of pretending that it was kind of interesting and undoubtedly healthy, it should have gone away.

But it hasn't. People have found new "uses" for it. Tofu ice cream, fried tofu, tofu underwear, and not one of these uses is any better than any of the others. None of them are any worse either. None of them are anything, just tofu. I, for one, am absolutely opposed to tofu. I think we should develop a campaign worldwide to ban it. Let's replace it with something that has a real personality.

How about goat cheese or fruit cocktail? You don't think of goat cheese as having no opinions. You know that goat cheese stands for something. It wouldn't allow itself to be made into ice cream. It would stand up and say, "Hell no!" You can trust goat cheese in a way that you could never trust tofu. You might not want to go where your goat cheese girlfriend wants to go, but at least you'd know where that is. You can offer alternatives to goat cheese's suggestions.

"I want to go out for Chinese food."

"Oh. I had Chinese for lunch. How about Korean? I could get some of that soup I like. You know, the kind without the tofu?"

Steal a Cadillac

Most of us try to practice some sort of moderation. We try to limit spending, lose a few pounds, view less television, whatever. Moderation produces a more balanced, healthy person. When we're moderate, we usually feel better about ourselves and, more in control of ourselves and the world around us. This feeling is, of course, an illusion, but not all illusions are bad. I can report from firsthand experience that three consecutive days of all-you-can-eat Indian buffets produce a longing for moderation, even if it isn't really evidence of my ability to control the workings of the universe.

By nature, I'm not a moderate person. I'm prone to obsessions, binges, and compulsions in lots of areas. I most assuredly eat too much, have owned perhaps three hundred bowling balls, don't drink a drop of alcohol (anymore), keep my books and music collections alphabetized, etc. etc. etc. I'd probably have to say that I'm past the middle of the road when it comes to going to extremes. Note that I said past the middle of the road and not over the edge of sanity. I think I fall well within a range of normal for the bulk of humanity.

What does this mean? How should this information help someone live a satisfactory life? First, accept yourself. You're probably normal, even though you know how strange you really are compared to other people you see around you. The ones who are capable of sustained moderation are the oddballs. They mow their lawns on time, change their oil every two thousand miles, eat two Oreos while watching the news, and run four miles three times a week. Their kids go to bed on time and never have tantrums in supermarkets. These are the strange ones who are perhaps best to avoid. They are likely to have freshly laid concrete floors in their basements and a missing elder relative. You, your life works, sort of, given a couple of well-placed patches and a truckload of guilt. Accept it as it is. That's the way the vast majority of us hope to make our lives work.

Once you've considered coming to grips with the fact that you're not going to be completely in control of anything important in life, then you can begin to fathom the strategy I've adopted. I say adopted because I most certainly didn't think of it on my own.

In 1968 I lived in a dorm at Boston College. It was a floor made up of a crop of future accountants and dentists who as of yet hadn't realized that exams on James Joyce or Existential Philosophy weren't going to be applied readily to their later endeavors. Most of us were buried in work as only Jesuits and particularly sadistic World War II Japanese prison guards were able to heap on.

Sometime around finals week, a few of us were talking about taking a short break. The popular consensus was to go to the cafeteria to grab a burger and look at the girls from the school of nursing. At this moment, a life-changing idea was presented by a guy named Dave.

Dave was one of the most anxious of us, always worrying that the dean would find out that he owned a car, and so he would lose his scholarship. The fact that the car was eleven years old and a hundred and fifty miles away was no comfort to him, as he stressed almost constantly.

Anyway, while trying to agree on a plan for escape from studying, Dave revealed a depth of character and wisdom none of us expected. His words were, and I quote: "If you're going to steal a car, steal a Cadillac." The importance of these words didn't immediately strike any of us. Dave said lots of things that we thought were nuts, so we kind of shrugged it off. The phrase was catchy, though, and it stuck with me somehow.

The trip to the cafeteria didn't have the desired effect. We found no real relief from the tension of studying, and in fact we were feeling guilty about the lost forty-five minutes. My college career became increasing colored by these feelings, which never fully succumbed to the alcohol treatment to which I submitted. I was a terrible student of the things they were trying to teach me, but I did learn some important lessons. Stealing Cadillacs is not the least among them.

The point is, as time passed, I learned that by cheating a little bit on moments of moderation, you still feel crappy about it, and you haven't truly enjoyed yourself. You return to the quest for a middle ground without having satisfied the urges that drove you away from your resolve in the first place.

Now, when I break my diet, I break it with nine donuts, instead of a granola bar. Those ridiculous low-cal, non-fat, sodium-free, carbless "foods" leave me craving and feeling guilty. An all-out onslaught on the buffet chain we affectionately call "The Trough" leaves me feeling like a leather-jacketed, motorcycle-riding rebel without a need to prove my manhood to anyone. My cravings are satisfied, and stay satisfied for long enough to have made a little progress in the weight loss quest. If, for some understandable reason, I don't lose the weight, I at least have enjoyed getting fat.

As Dave's father had said to him: if he ever was called by the police to pick him up after having stolen a car, it had damned well better be a Cadillac.

Lost and Found

I tried to write a story. I've always loved fiction, and I've secretly wanted to really take a stab at this endeavor. I mean *great* fiction. I want people to speak about me behind my back, saying that I'm brilliant, that I move them with my elegant and poignant stories, that I have a great heart along with an astounding mind. I want them to try to be seen with me, so that their friends will be impressed. I intend to oblige all who have these longings. I don't plan to be aloof about this stuff, but rather to be as warm and generous once I'm famous as I am now. Anyway, I got this new laptop computer for my sixtieth birthday, and I started to write a story.

The story was in the finest tradition of over-the-top melodrama. In it, a rugged but sensitive man (patterned after myself) is tragically widowed by a traffic accident. In addition to losing his beloved wife (think Loretta Young here, or if you're not old enough to remember her, Meryl Streep), his young son is also killed in the accident. To cope with this capricious twist, our hero moves away to the area in which he was raised, near the banks of the Connecticut River, buys an old farm, and applies himself to singlehandedly rebuilding the barn into one of those *Architectural Digest* places that no one could really afford.

He adopts a German shepherd, who romps across the place and who eventually leads our hero to meet a lonely but honorable boy fishing along the aforementioned river. In a noble gesture, he tells the kid to leave the premises (in the interest of safety, of course), and the kid responds with curious resignation. The reason for the curious resignation was just about to be revealed by a mystery woman who was pulling into the driveway of our palace-in-progress when my computer went down.

I've made it clear in the past that I pride myself on technical ignorance. I've cultivated it carefully and used it at many parties and gatherings to impress others. It's part of the devil-may-care persona I've built up over a lifetime. I take great pleasure in the looks I get when I tell people that I keep my cell phone turned off and in my car. I can barely contain myself when I let it slip that I have a blog but I can't find it. I think it gives people hope to see someone like me. I'm inspiring.

Anyway, my computer went down just at the moment the potential love interest and salvation was about to reach our hero. Of course, I hadn't bothered to back up the document. (I think that's the phrase that means to do something to make sure you don't lose important things on your computer.) Yet I take heart that it might still be in there somewhere. After all, where could it go?

The pleasant young man from India or Indonesia or wherever he was from who tried to talk me through the steps required to get things going again didn't take it, although lord knows he had enough time to. Two and a half hours of unplugging, holding resets, counting to fifty before letting go, and trying to insert cables into cliff faces seven hundred feet above the ground finally resulted in his having to do the unthinkable. He had to speak to a supervisor ("Please to hold on to the phone for a brief while. I must speak to a supervisor about this.") A brief while in Sri Lanka or Xanadu or wherever he was from is apparently enough time for the neighbor's elephant to become impregnated, progress through gestation, and give birth.

It should be noted here that while all this holding on was going on, the phone was beeping into my ear. The beeping was only occasional at first, but was becoming progressively more insistent and regular as Dumbo was being seen on ultrasound photos. My wife, who was now home from work, informed me that the beeping was a signal that the phone's batteries were dying. I was now in a race against time. If the phone died while I was on hold, the entire process would be for naught. I was suddenly reminded of those movies starring Bruce Willis or Keanu Reeves, where some insane guy rigs up a bomb in a hospital or pet shop, and the hero has a very limited time to find and defuse it. Would the elephant get born before the phone gave up the ghost?

Well, our hero returned from his trip to the mountaintop with news from his supervisor. "I'm very sorry to say that the equipment is broken, sir. If you would like to send it to us, we will repair or replace it and send it back to you when the process is completed. By the way, Rajid's elephant is the proud mother of a four-hundred-pound baby girl, who we would like to honor by naming her after you."

Well, not to be stymied by the Third World, I trotted myself out in a snowstorm to my neighborhood Staples. With my busted router in hand, I prepared to buy a new one, install it, and proceed to introduce my hero to the social worker who was about to save his soul and the soul of the little boy by the river.

Now, Staples is a kind of pet peeve of mine. It seems like it's one of those things that are lately taking over the world as I know it. There must be one of them on every street corner. One day you have a hardware store run by some fat, bald guy named Ray, and the next day it's a Staples. Unlike fat, bald Ray, Staples has no soul. The people working there are probably nice enough in their real lives. I'm sure they mow their lawns and make casseroles just like everyone else. It's just that once they get to work, they seem to change.

The biggest change I see is blindness. You just can't get seen in a Staples. I wandered up and down the aisle that sold routers, trying to read boxes and look needy. When that failed to bring help, I went to the checkout area, expecting to find someone there who knew something about what they were selling. Nice-looking, middle aged ladies waved packages over bar code readers, but none of them knew anything at all about routers. The tech guy was on the phone (just like I had been the day before). This could take hours. All I needed was fifteen seconds, and I was going to get it—in about an hour.

I didn't have it in me to deal with this, so I put it back on the shelf and headed for Best Buy. Best Buy has nothing but technicians and one girl who worked the checkout counter. I had to fight my way through a wall of technicians, all telling dirty Microsoft jokes that only they could understand, but I ended up with the same router I'd had at Staples and at the same price.

Now, installing a router is pretty much a mechanical process. Basic mechanics I can handle. Two phone jacks and a power cord, and the new router was in place. The only issue was that the computer still didn't work.

I don't handle frustration well. I can take a certain amount of it, and then I just have to smack something. I was in definite smacking territory now, but I had to keep it together, because I had to make another phone call. The router wasn't the answer, so now I had to deal with *the modem*. With the modem came a call to COMCAST.

Come to find out, COMCAST is in Texas or Louisiana or someplace else. They own the modem, and we just kind of rent it. Without it, we can't get internet service. Just because internet service isn't cheap doesn't mean it's not unreliable. That, however, is not the reason it isn't in the story I was trying to find in some cybercloset. I didn't put it in my story because my main character had suffered enough with the loss of his family. Having to deal with the internet would have been just too cruel.

Anyway, after a deep breath, I called the 800 number on the receipt I found. There was the requisite pressing of numbers before I could speak to a person. Once that hurdle was passed, I found myself on the line with a nine-year-old girl from somewhere where they spoke with a Southern accent. "How're y'all doon today?" This girl was asking the wrong person.

"Not too well. I just got back from driving in a snowstorm to get a router, but that still didn't fix my computer. I was on the line for two hours before that, getting help to get back online, but my computer still won't work."

"Really, y'all got snow? We don't git snow heah. I seen it once when I was visitin' my aunt and uncle in North Dakota, but I was real little and I can hardly remember it."

What was I hearing? What did she just say? "Excuse me? Do you know anything about computers, because that's why I called. The snow sucks. It's just there for me to have to dig out once I get off the phone with you, because I think the chances of you being able to fix this computer are about the same as my being able to fly to the moon by flapping my arms. I'm going to dig out of the snow and drive to the nearest computer store and throw myself off the roof."

"Would y'all like me to look up the location of the nearest computer store, sir? I know y'all don't have internet, and I can tell by the beeping that your phone battery's going dead."

Unholy Wedlock

I'm a big fan of marriage. I've actually done it twice myself, and though the first time didn't work out, I still like the institution very much. I know that there are many different kinds of marriages, and I'm guessing that even those that we think are strange, like arranged marriages or polygamy, have some things to recommend them. I just like the idea of adults making commitments. We should stand firm somewhere, put it on the line, and that's what I think marriage is about.

I have to admit to some confusion about the recent controversy about the definition of marriage. Is there someone who doesn't know what marriage is? I, for one, can't remember when I didn't know what it was. I know I might be slipping, but I still think I do. I must admit, though, that once you try to explain it, it becomes more elusive. It's like scratching an itch. You contort yourself to get at one, and it seems to move to another spot. It's easy to recognize, but not to pin down. In any case, I basically think that most things competent adults do in the privacy of their own homes are their business. I have plenty to do to keep my own insanity in check.

Well, that's not really what I'm bent out of shape about. The marriages that I think are perversions have to do with food. For the last few weeks, a local donut chain has been advertising a new item: a sausage wrapped in a pancake. They fill their front windows with an enormous photo of two or three of these Frankensteinian foods, one of which appears to have been bitten into. There has to be one of these, otherwise you wouldn't have real proof that there actually is a sausage in there. I'm sure that the chain hired a food stylist to lay them out, stacking and turning them so that they could put their best foot forward. To me, they look like autopsy photos.

I love pancakes, and I love sausages. I like link sausages, patties, kielbasa, chorizo, Italian sausage (both sweet and hot), hot dogs, and any other kind of sausage I can think of. I even have an occasional yen for a Slim Jim, but there is something revolting about this pancake concoction. I think it should be banned. I think whoever thought of it should be condemned for taking pleasing and humble foods and twisting them into an unnatural abomination. I hope to all that's holy that whoever is in charge of this company will get treatment for the employee who did this.

I know that this might be thought of as a digression, but what's the story with food stylists, anyway? What kind of a world do we live in when someone can make their living making food into a decoration? I heard they use white glue for milk, because milk isn't white enough. If that's true, I think we have another example of our preference for sizzle over steaks. I hope to god that the cows don't find out. Can you imagine how hurt they'd be? I guess in our down economy, we should be creative about jobs, but as soon as things get a little better, the Department of Agriculture should go after these "stylists" for defamation of dairy products or something.

While I'm on the subject, I'd like to get something else off my chest. I think that vegetarian products that are made to look and taste like meats pander to those who should be eating meat. I'm not saying that vegetarians are wrong or bad. I tried it in the seventies and didn't like it. I claimed that I felt better, healthier, and more moral, but really all I was trying to do was impress hippie girls. I wasn't all that cute and I had trouble keeping myself angry enough to appeal to the political chicks, so I stopped eating meat. It turned out that it wasn't as stupid as it sounds, but it still was pretty suspect. I didn't meet any new girls, and I really missed out on lots of meaty delights.

Anyway, I've had a couple of recent run-ins with people eating tofurkey and tofu hot dogs. They acted holier than thou, because they weren't eating any of our four-legged brethren. I have some strange family members, but none have four legs. It really irked me. If you're going to eat something that looks and tastes like meat, eat meat. If you're going to be vegetarian, commit yourself to it and do it. It's like marriage. It's not so important to whom you commit yourself, but that you do so with clear eyes and real intent. Then let the pancakes fall where they may.

Driving at Night

I'm getting old. I don't mean I'm getting older, I'm getting old. My hair has been graying for years, my once better-than-perfect eyes are behind "progressive lenses," I have pains that are so chronic they seem like old friends, and I have old friends who are chronic pains. There are lots of other signs that I notice. I got a dental bridge last year. After a lifetime of dental phobia, coupled with the magical thought that finally I'd deal with my dozen cavities and cracking fillings, I finally surrendered. I went to the dentist that my wife recommended, and laid it on the line. I told him that I knew my teeth were bad, and I knew that I needed plenty of money and time to invest in this process, and that I wouldn't ever really do what was necessary to make them right again.

Now I recognize that moment as a sign of maturity. I had given up on the fantasy that I would somehow do the grown-up thing and attend the jillion appointments that would be made in order to make it all right. The dentist sent me to another dentist, who went through the whole thing with me again. This time I was better prepared to handle it, and I laid out the situation right off the bat. I told him I would intend to do right, would even make it to the first two appointments. I would reschedule the third and get to that appointment. I would cancel the fourth in the evening, leaving a message with the answering service, and say that I would call back to make another, but I wouldn't get around to it.

This wasn't a plan. I didn't sit down and make this up. I'd just gone through it a hundred times with myself, and I had absolutely no reason to think that this time I was going to be different. I laid all this out to dentist number two, and he leaned against his instrument cabinet and smiled. He was clearly refreshed by my candor, and he gave me the straightforward facts about dental implants and bridges. The bridge would require many fewer appointments. That was the decider for me. I had my two bad teeth pulled, strapped on my bridge, and have moved on in a new direction.

I don't take pride in having poor dental hygiene. I'm not saying that a bridge is as good as my own teeth were. It's not. There are things I can't enjoy the way I once did, but I don't get toothaches anymore. What I do feel some satisfaction about is that I made a mature decision. I'm getting old, and I don't feel so strongly that I have to put on a good face for others. It's a relief to admit that I won't do the hard things, so I might as well do the next best things and move on.

Before I go any further, I want to be clear that I am the world's most married man. I'm completely happy in my life, and I have zero interest in doing anything that would change even the least pleasing part of it. That being said, being old has other advantages. When I was younger, I enjoyed looking at women. I still enjoy it, but there's a lovely difference. In my twenties, there were very few really attractive girls. Most had some glaring flaw that marred their appearance, a failing that I couldn't fully overlook. These days, there are very few women that I see that don't have at least one feature that I find pleasantly attractive to look at. It's a most delightful juxtaposition. Not only is my view immensely improved, but I even get the feeling that my glaring flaws may not be so bad. When I look at the other guys my age, I figure I'm okay.

Several years ago, our family flew to Chicago for a reunion with Marcie's relatives. She comes from a small family, with only a couple of cousins, and they are pretty close despite living thousands of miles apart. The occasion was the fiftieth anniversary of her aunt and uncle. There was plenty of fun at the hotel for the dozen or so kids who attended. I really like Marcie's family, and her brother, her cousin Gary and I hung out watching sports, eating nachos and telling stupid jokes. Overall, it was just the kind of party I like most.

The big event was a dinner for the anniversary couple. We all sat at a table with probably thirty people of all ages, seated roughly according to blood ties and age. I noticed a very handsome older man sitting beside Marcie's aunt. He looked very much like a shorter, eighty-year-old version of Kirk Douglas. The next morning, I asked Cousin Gary who he was. Gary instantly lost his smile. He growled that he was his mother's brother, and that he wasn't a very nice man. Gary went on to say that he was a widower who lived in Florida for most of the year.

The thing that Gary found so distasteful about him was that he was enjoying a kind of sexual awakening in his declining years, and he really liked telling his nephew about his exploits. Gary couldn't deter him from this, no matter what he said. The man was apparently a huge hit with the widows in his condo complex. These were all women who had been cautious and demure when younger, but now, what the hell. He told Gary the secret of his success. "Gary, if you can hear and drive at night, you've got it made!"

By that set of standards, I'm screwed. My hearing is one of my worst features. Some time ago I noticed that I had to ask to have things repeated, sometimes several times. Most people are indulgent about such things, but after a while, they get frustrated. Incessant huhs or wha's just seem to irritate those being asked to say again that which they've just said before.

I should admit that I've never been that attentive. I sometimes have to have things repeated because I wasn't listening, but this is different. In fact, the harder I listen, the more likely I am to have to have things said again. I'm told that this is a pattern in men of my age. Ambient noise appears to be much louder, and the particular words or sounds you're trying to hear get drowned out.

Lately I've developed a new strategy to deal with this issue. When I'm told something I don't hear, I repeat something that might sound like what was said, but in fact couldn't possibly have been said. For example, if a student of mine says that they'd like permission to get a glass of water, I might repeat "You say you want to eat a blotter?" This works a little better because it amuses the repeater enough to be willing to try again. Additionally, it makes it clear that they are dealing with someone who might be senile. That triggers sympathy and sometimes a little anxiety that I might become violent if frustrated. Marcie has suggested (rather strongly, I might add) that I get a hearing aid. Maybe someday. Right now I'm having fun making things up to say.

Now, there are many things about being old that I don't like. If I could drop thirty years right now, I most probably would do it, but there is a part of me that would hesitate. I think we have our path to follow, and we do it to the best of our ability. We make mistakes that can't be corrected, and possibly shouldn't be. They are part of the fabric of who we are.

In retrospect, being young wasn't all that wonderful. There were worries about what I looked like that I've pretty much overcome. There was the difficulty of pleasing our parents, teachers, friends, and just about everyone else we met. I still like to be liked, but not enough to work at it. I feel bad about some things sometimes, but I forget pretty quickly. *Bonanza* and *All in the Family* reruns are readily available on YouTube and various other sources, so whenever I want to feel young again, I can. I don't look forward to losing any more of my health than I already have, but I'm going to a yearly physical and more or less holding my own.

Twenty-five years ago, a mentor of mine told me that she enjoyed her grown children because they had so much to talk about. I've begun to see what she meant by that, and I can imagine when I'll have grandchildren. I guess that we have our place and time in the great scheme of things, and mine has been a good one so far. After all, being old isn't being dead.

Character Flaws

I saw a disturbing thing today. I was at a meeting at work, one of those long sessions with a dozen or so people, one of whom thinks to bring a snack for everyone. It's a nice gesture, thoughtful and worthy of praise. On this occasion, one of my colleagues brought a box of assorted chocolates. I happen to work with a special group of people, universally likeable and competent. That's why I was so disappointed by what I saw. One of the women politely took the box as it circled the room, checked the underside of the lid to find the kind she wanted, and picked that particular chocolate. I was revolted.

Is there a worse feeling than that which occurs when someone for whom you had respect reveals such a moral lapse? My mood turned from focused and productive to furious about the conditions under which we now live. I was saddened and embarrassed for the moral weakness, the inability to commit, the reluctance to face the future that this act represented. What happened to the spirit Americans used to have when we chose chocolates randomly? What about the ability to take a chance, facing the consequences of our choices with courage?

When I was a kid, we took our chocolates as they came. Oh sure, we knew that most of the round ones were soft centers, the quadrilaterals hard, but we learned that through trial and error. We took responsibility for our choices and ate some we didn't want. Those difficult days made us strong, developed our character, and made us the kind of Americans that built our country.

As I processed the outrage, I was at once flooded by other examples of this sad decline. My own wife, usually a real risk taker, carefully handpicks the black jelly beans from our Easter candy. Now, I'm not only complaining because it changes the time-honored ratio of blacks to reds (her least favorite color), but because this kind of selfishness is becoming more and more a part of our daily lives. Everywhere you look, you see people who are so absorbed in their own narrow interests that they won't let you into a line of traffic, hog the armrest at the movie theater, and a hundred other indignities we hardly notice, but which contribute to a meaner, more isolated world. I really believe this is part of a loosely organized but extremely effective pattern designed to play on our curiosity and insecurity in order to enrich any number of industries.

As a species, our desire to know is unparalleled. The best man at my wedding is a sophisticated native of New York City. Highly educated and urbane, he was teaching at Harvard Medical School when we first met. He had moved into an apartment above us in a multi-family unit, and he popped in to introduce himself. He was all Manhattan silk until I asked him what he did. His eyes got a little glassy and he said, "I'm a gleal man."

He said it like everyone should know exactly what that meant, like everyone fell into the category of gleal man or non-gleal man. I weighed the plusses and minuses of asking the obvious question. Do I ask, and risk traumatizing him with the fact that not everyone was into gleal, or do I just keep going and hope the subject didn't come up again? Anyway, I asked and found out that gleal has something to do with fat in the cells or some such thing.

The point is that as a species, we want to know about everything, even gleal. This quality has probably always been exploited, but never more than today. I think the medical field is one of the biggest offenders. My friend just had a baby. Like lots of others, she *had to* know the gender before he was born. I can't really criticize that, because we did the same thing when our daughter was born. After all, what if you got a blue blanket by accident? It's kind of like checking the lid on the box of chocolates.

A few years ago, I heard lots of ads for full-body scans. These were designed to test your body for every possible health risk, you know, early detection stuff. It was a good moneymaker, especially given the fear factor so carefully nurtured into our daily lives. The equipment was available and the technicians were probably just hanging around drinking decaf or something. Why not make a few bucks while waiting for sick people? From what I understand, insurance companies went ballistic. Suddenly, frantic people were screaming for more tests to diagnose reasons for malformed arterial whatchamacallits or under-developed renal doohickeys.

Can you imagine, entrepreneurial medicine coming into financial conflict with the medical insurance industry? Not since King Kong versus Godzilla have two more powerful and potentially malevolent forces met in combat. I'm not sure of the details, but those ads seem to have stopped. Now, if only we could find a worthy opponent for the chocolate box cartel.

The Best and the Brightest

I've become wary of adjectives. Lately, I seem to be seeing lots of them, and I'm wondering why. They remind me of those scenes in western movies, when the outlaw gang moseys into town in ones and twos. They try to look inconspicuous as they wait for the leader's signal to rob the bank. Once they're pointed out, it becomes obvious that they're up to no good. That's why I'm uncomfortable with adjectives.

The first I remember seeing them was on menus. It wasn't any big thing, you know, home-cooked pies, stuff like that. It wasn't information that was suspicious. As we got used to that, someone upped the ante with items like 100% all-beef. At first glance, that seems like hearty goodness, but on closer inspection, it's a bit alarming. What were they serving before their hamburgers were 100% all-beef? What was the beef percentage relative to the whatever else percentage? To be honest, questions like that have only come to me now that the bank may be in imminent danger.

Next adjectives began to branch out into the sociopolitical adjectives. Free range chickens have become all the rage. Every time I see that advertised, I picture the old West, with chicken roundups, branding chickens, chicken stampedes, chicken rustlers, and all the rest. I have a once-suppressed memory of one my uncles catching one of the free range chickens he used to keep around his yard, twisting its neck, and plucking it for a cookout. Free ranging did that chicken very little good.

I don't deny that we should be aware of the cost of eating whatever we eat. Something has to die for us to live. We should be appreciative of that, but I, for one, don't need to know where the chicken lived that I'm eating.

Menus haven't been the last stop for this adjective infestation. We have fair-trade stuff now, renewable-resource napkins, high-octane low-emission fuels, hypoallergenic makeup, and all kind of gradations, manifestations, and permutations of things that used to be pretty straightforward. I long for things that can be described simply as small, medium, or large.

As the adjectives have been insinuating themselves further and further into our everyday lives, I notice that they've been morphed into a kind of Frankensteinian distortion of things that were perfectly okay before, but are now new and improved into something unrecognizable.

One of the big moments of my life came behind the candy counter of my family's grocery store. It happened the day M&M's introduced peanuts into their confection. There was room in my life for both, but was there need? M&M's were the perfect candy. They came in pieces, so that if you had to share them with your sister, you could measure out the correct numbers. They came in bright colors that all tasted exactly the same. They melted in your mouth, not in your hand. What more did you need?

Coffee used to come black. You could add milk or sugar. Some people added a lot of milk, some none; some people used lump sugar, others granulated. Then came decaf, and the walls came tumbling down. What do caramel or mocha or espresso shots have to do with coffee? Some places now make us order our coffee in some other language. It sounds like Italian, but who knows?

I'm beginning to think that it's all part of some mindless lemming hike into a maze of possibilities that didn't have to exist, but now seem so important that we can't live without them. The adjectives are designed to separate one insignificant product from another insignificant product, so that we select the one they want us to select. The hidden danger is the growing feeling that we've made the wrong choice. We walk away with bent shoulders and careworn faces, thinking that we should have gone with the cappuccino. We imagine that the world is chuckling behind our backs as we get into our Lexus (I should have got the hybrid) and curse our mocha latte.

The free market, it turns out, is far from free. The finest minds available have taken up the task of convincing us that we need things that didn't exist yesterday. No wonder stress and anxiety is the disaster of the day. Me, I'm not a lot better than anybody else. Personally, I think Double Stuff Oreos are the best thing since chocolate milk.

Capital Punishment

Recently I drove Marcie to the airport. She and two friends were on their way to Paris to meet my daughter, who was returning from a semester in South Africa. No trip to any airport is for the faint of heart, and when we go, just to make it more interesting, there's usually some special degree of difficulty. I thought this trip would be straightforward. The plan was to get the crew there by six in the evening for an eight o'clock flight.

Now, giving someone a ride to the airport is the greatest favor that can ever be done. Given a choice, it's less painful to donate a kidney without anesthetic than to give a ride to the airport. In the sequence of favors, throwing yourself on a live grenade is just behind giving someone a ride to the airport. This is especially true during rush hour, which this clearly was. In my mind, it was a profound demonstration of love, but given that I would soon be seeing my daughter for the first time in six months and that my wife would be gone for ten days, it seemed like the right thing to do.

Despite the inherent difficulty, I was confident that it could be done. I left work at three and headed in a homeward direction. I needed to stop for gas, visit an ATM, and take a shower. There was no reason not to believe that all this and more could be accomplished. As usual, I'd gone over the whole thing in my head at least fifty times, and it always went off without a hitch. The gas station should have been a hint of what was to come.

I never let my car go below half a tank. I know its neurotic, but it just makes me uncomfortable to let it go. It's only one of the little oddities I live with. I don't expect others to live my way, not anymore. Thirty years of marriage has smoothed the edges of unreasonable expectations. I don't have to do lots of stuff Marcie thinks is important, and she doesn't have to do my stuff. For example, we have two cars. Hers is perpetually a third of a millimeter from empty, and mine is rarely below three-quarters full.

Before it sounds like my only flaw is excessive responsibility, I run out of medications for blood pressure and cholesterol, don't make dentist appointments, pay bills or call my mother. I put off grocery shopping and brushing the dogs. I'm a year behind on renewing their licenses. My mail goes unopened, and I never answer the phone. I could go on, but I think you get it.

The point is, this one time, I had less than a quarter of a tank. That never happens. I had been really tired the day before, and knowing I had time after work, I let it go. I went over the calculations in my head a dozen times. Eleven miles to work, another mile to the station on my way home. I knew the needle would be below the quarter mark, the great uncharted last region of the tank. It disturbed my sleep, knowing that the gauge was so low, but for this one time, after all my calculations, I took the chance.

Anyway, on the way home after work, I stopped at a little gas station I know, put down the window, and waited. The guy came over and began to stammer. It seems he had nothing but high-test to serve. High-test, and oil at something like eleven thousand dollars a barrel. I'd just been paid, but who can tell if two weeks' salary could fill more than three-quarters of a tank with high-test? I could always give them my gold watch if twelve hundred dollars in the bank account didn't cover it.

The little wheels on the pump began to spin. They were going so fast I swear they were smoking. When I was sixteen, for a week's work at my family's grocery store I got a twenty-dollar bill and the use of our 1966 Buick. I was to use the twenty to fill it up, and I could keep the change. That Buick was as big as an auditorium. It must have had a thousand-gallon tank, but I could fill it up, and with the change, take my girlfriend to the movies. Watching the blur of numbers, I thought of that Buick.

Anyway, I filled the tank—thankfully without having to bargain away any family heirlooms—and headed for my next errand. I had to stop at an ATM to get cash. I live in the suburbs; there are ATM's everywhere. Park the car, in and out two minutes later, and home for a break. A reasonable plan, which of course had no chance to go as expected.

I made it into the bank, and there was one guy in front of me at the ATM. He was carefully reading the screen. I mean c-a-r-e-f-u-l-l-y reading the screen. When he finally got it down, he began pressing the requisite button. That led to a new screen and another c-a-r-e-f-u-l reading.

In situations like this, the best part of my character tells me to be patient, to take the moment to consider the mysteries of the universe, count my blessings, try to remember a recipe for stuffed bell peppers I once saw. The best part of my character tells me that all of god's creatures have their own ways and that all ways are worthy of god's love. The best part of my character tells me that my errand is, after all, infinitely small in the face of eternity. All of this is supposed to add up to love for the guy in front of me at the ATM. Good wishes for the task he faces, and the rest of the day ahead for both of us.

The problem is that the best part of my character is about 3 percent of the total. The other 97 percent was beginning to get prickly. My predecessor was punching buttons now, each one producing a distinctive electronic buzz, but each one at least fifteen minutes apart from the one before it. What in god's name was he doing? From the rear, he didn't seem enfeebled. He seemed to have all the normal abilities needed to get a twenty-dollar bill from his account and to get the hell out of my way.

I was watching a nearby hilltop as it eroded into a river valley when I heard the repeated ringing of the little bell that means a receipt has been printed and was now waiting in the slot to be picked up. My heart began to beat more quickly. The bell continued to chirp, and still he stood there. Trees outside budded and flowered, the leaves changed color, and fell. He finally took the receipt and began to read.

It wasn't exactly *War and Peace*. Two, maybe three lines of dull transaction—how long could it take? It snowed, plows came, the snow banks got dirty with road dirt, and they melted. At last, the ATM was making the other sound it makes when your card has been ejected after your transaction. You then take it and go. Take it and go. *Take it and go!* Still he stood. The junior teller in the bank completed thirty-five years of service, had a retirement party, and left. The man took the card, faked a shoulder as if to go, stopped, turned back to the ATM, and put the card back in.

There are moments of insight in life. They come at odd times, about surprising things. Often they come in the midst of everyday experiences, things you've done a hundred times, but one time when you do them, something changes, and it's never the same again. Such was the moment when he put the card back in.

For years, I've spoken against capital punishment. It's not that I don't think there are people who deserve it. There are. It's rather that I think it hurts the rest of society to participate in a killing. At once, in the moment he put the card back in, I felt an almost overwhelming urge to strangle him from behind. I've seen it done on television and in movies. Just wrap a forearm around his neck and hang on for a while.

Of course I'd never do it, but the fantasy has its purpose. Imagining something can serve to allow us not to have to do it in actuality. I wallowed in the dream, but I didn't do it. What I did was to walk out in a huff. I went to the supermarket next door, and in ninety seconds, I had my cash.

Now I do have a few ideas about how to deal with ATM felonies like I'd just experienced. How about programming the machine to give an electric shock to anyone who exceeds one transaction or whose transaction takes more than, say, five minutes? What if, after five minutes, the machine shreds your card and you forfeit your money? What if it went one step further and gave your money to the next person in line? What if it emitted a puff of some toxic gas that paralyzes the guy who's messing everything up and lets you take your turn? All worthy ideas that I intend to suggest to my congressman.

At any rate, with my money in hand, I headed home and then to the airport. As I pulled into my driveway at four o'clock, I saw Marcie sprinting out the back door. When she saw me, she began to babble breathlessly. "Hurry! Hurry! Kathy is coming! The plane is at 6:30, not 8:00! We have to go! I'll drive! I'll drive!" At that moment, the best part of my character told me to be patient.

Fifty Steps

Update.

I've been learning a lot lately. It's not that I've been trying to learn more, rather, life has been giving me lessons unasked for. I'm thinking that it has to do with the stage of life I'm going through. I'm due to turn sixty in three days. They say that sixty is the new forty, but since I'm not new myself, sixty feels like the old sixty to me. I've lived through childhood (mostly), young adulthood, "maturity," and now I'm preparing to be old. Before you begin to think that I'm lamenting that, I consider myself lucky. That gets me to the lessons.

Over the past eight months, I've lost two friends to pancreatic cancer. Neither was as old as me. The first was Diane. She was a beautiful woman. A Southern belle who had it all: a PhD, a doting MD husband, two great kids, everything. Everything, that is, including cancer. She lasted nearly a year after her diagnosis. She fought every minute, trying every procedure, so that she could hold out to see all the big things coming to her: her daughter marry, her son graduate from college, the birth of grandchildren, anniversaries, birthdays, you know the things I mean.

Through it all, she held on to a grace that I can't manage on my best day. She kept a sense of humor that was aimed to keep those of us around her comfortable in her presence. Near the end, she and her husband had a conversation about her funeral. He asked her what she thought of cremation. She said she was "warming to the idea."

Lesson learned: you live better when you think of others.

Fifty Steps

Just about three weeks ago, our friend Steve died. Like Diane, he was probably the last person of our age group you'd expect to die. He was a black belt ex-Marine who never sat still. He coached the girls' soccer team, bounced on neighborhood trampolines, and began each day asking his wife, "What are we going to do today?" He was a kid magnet who outplayed six-year-olds with regularity, and it was never forced with Steve. He had a kid's capacity for finding pleasure in the simplest motion.

There was plenty about Steve that wasn't just play. He was a brilliant engineer who had security clearances to work on projects no one ever heard about. He tried bull riding, traveled to the Amazon, and was a son, father, brother, and husband, but he died just a few short months after being diagnosed. Steve decided to try chemotherapy, and if that didn't work, he'd go for the best months he could. He didn't want to stretch his life by adding weeks or months of misery.

I'm not one to push into places where I'm not wanted, and cancer scares me. Steve and his family were pretty self-contained. I was ready to say all the right things, right from my living-room couch. My wife, Marcie, however, was at their door. She came home and told me Steve was asking for me, so now I had to go.

The thing that was shocking was that Steve was still Steve. He was thinner, granted, and his color wasn't good, but he was still Steve. He didn't want to talk about cancer, he wanted to talk car repairs and the Red Sox, and he stayed that way. Even after he had a stroke, he was still Steve.

He even told me that he was lucky. He'd seen people at the hospital who had no one with them. He worried about how they could live with cancer without friends and family around them. It gave him an idea. He would run a marathon. It would be in a wheelchair, and so it would require help. That was the beauty of the plan. He didn't want anyone to have to provide lots of help.

Steve knew that no one was going to be able to push him twenty-six miles any more than someone would be able to cure his cancer. His idea was to have ordinary people push him for fifty steps each. Enough ordinary people could contribute fifty steps and so complete a marathon. For Steve it was a metaphor. You don't cure pancreatic cancer, but you can defeat it. You defeat it by continuing to live your life even though you're ill. Steve did that, and he knew that living didn't have to mean bull riding. It could mean sharing soup and telling bad jokes, things he did right until the end.

Lesson learned: we all can walk fifty steps, and we all can do little things that make all the difference.

Made in the USA
Charleston, SC
09 July 2012